TEACHING OF BIOLOGY

TEACHING OF BIOLOGY

Dr. Archana Tomar

KALPAZ PUBLICATIONS
Delhi-110052

Teaching of Biology

ISBN: 81-7835-327-X

Published in 2005 in India by
Kalpaz Publications,
C-30, Satyawati Nagar, Delhi-110052
E-mail : Kalpaz@hotmail.com

Laser Typesetting at : Shiva Infosystem, Delhi
Printed at : Mehra Offset Press, Delhi

Contents

	Foreword	7
	Preface	11
	Acknowledgements	15
1.	Nature and Scope of Biology	17
2.	Objectives of Teaching Biology	29
3.	Biology and Correlation	49
4.	Instructional Planning	53
5.	Methods of Teaching	69
6.	Approach	99
7.	Models of Teaching	123
8.	Laboratory	151
9.	Curriculum Organisation	169
10.	Teaching Aids	193
11.	Learning Biology Through Activities	207
12.	Evaluation	241
	Bibliography	261
	Index	269

Foreword

One of the time-honoured goals of general education is to produce the intellectually and mentally, spiritually, emotionally, ethically and morally sound human. Man is a thinking creature-rational animal by virtue of his intellect and reason, or what the philosophers call rational faculty. Sound and excellent intellect is one which possesses the capacity to know and understand the principles of many kinds of things, as opposed to having a quantitatively massive amount of informative data about particular thing. Students in the school need to be exposed to knowledge of general principles of things than are currently the case, and of how these diverse principles might be applied to diverse situations and instances.

To attain the comprehension of complex phenomenon of the objective world by the students, the teacher, in some cases, has to apply the principle of historicism while explaining the processes of natural and social life development. The elements of historicism in the process of explaining scientific theories, main laws and general notions of a life make it possible for student to understand the constant broadening of the limits of cognition; continuous transition from limited and restricted knowledge to a fuller and more profound knowledge. Under the conditions of school teaching there is little chance for a profound study of history of scientific notions, and their emergence and development. We can only select the most important facts of the historical development of some doctrines, general notions, connecting short inroads into the past with modern state and prospects of scientific cognition.

Improving the educational process, progressive schools and teachers have increased the proportion of independent work of students; laboratory and practical, educational experiments etc. Parallel with the lesson, which is the main form of educational process of nature, to museums, to historical to cultural monuments etc., educational and field trips. The later are the reflections of teaching of biology itself, as it provides a possibility of revealing correctly, the objective laws of reality in the course of cognition. Thus practicing technical arts and agricultural experimental work, school children learn to apply the knowledge, to enrich it and to master the creative ways of cognitive activities.

In India science is a compulsory subject for the first ten years of schooling. This has been done with a clear objective. The main emphasis at secondary level is to (i) Make learners capable of taking part in activities related to areas of food, agriculture, health, environmental protection, energy, wild-life management, social forestry, nutrition industry and shelter; and (ii) Develop a scientific temper and attitude to live more effectively as a responsible citizen. For these, learners should be acquainted with the nature of scientific knowledge, concepts of science, processes of science, value relationships between science and technology and society and acquire skills to use tools, apparatus, instruments and equipments.

For attaining the above objectives, there is a need to emphasize the functional aspects of scientific knowledge and of skills. At this stage, the pupils will gradually be able to think logically in terms of hypothetical solutions relevant to particular problem. For this reason child should be encouraged to think in terms of abstract situations.

When gradually science education is taking a back seat in India, where less number of students opt for sciences at the undergraduate level. The students are not opting for science course. This book will be valuable for teachers to educate the students about nature and scope of biology and various avenues, which can be explored. It will educate the teachers and students about various approaches that can be used to make biology teaching interesting. The knowledge should be broad based and as far as possible it must be taught in an integrated and interdisciplinary manner.

Dr. Archana Tomar has written a book on teaching of biology, which will be a good resource material for the teacher educators and B. Ed students. It covers number of things from objectives, method, media, approaches, models, use of teaching aids, evaluation and activity to teach science in general and biology in particular. It will be useful for the researchers in the area of classroom instruction. I congratulate Dr. Archana Tomar for her contribution in the field of Education.

Prof. K. C. Upadhyay
Vice Chancellor
The Maharaja Sayajirao University of Baroda
Baroda

Preface

Science Education in general and biology education in particular is passing through a strange phase. Science is used in every phase of day, it has made our life so comfortable. It is a strange phenomena to see that there are very few takers of science today at the graduate and the post graduate level. So much so that UGC had to announce special scheme to attract the students at the master degree. Some-where the strength is getting reduced at the school level, which gets translated into choice at the higher education level. In this book attempt has been made to make biology teaching more interesting and live.

It takes of with the first unit, which talks about the Nature and scope of biology at the plus two stage. In this unit attempt has been made to make the reader understand about nature of biology, various avenues available after studying biology, research institutes working for training and development of biology.

Next comes the objectives, which have to be achieved by teaching of biology. These are further classified into cognitive, affective and psychomotor. The revised Blooms taxonomy also finds place in this chapter.

Objectives of teaching biology are followed by correlation in biology. Any subject cannot be taught in a compartmentalized manner, it has to lend support to other subject and similarly it has to take support from other subjects.

Planning of instruction in an academic year follows correlation. Three types of planning are taken up in a year, annual planning, unit planning and lesson planning.

All the three types of planning have been discussed with suitable illustrations.

Next to appear are the methods of teaching biology. The methods have been classified into three types. Teacher centred methods, Pupil centred methods and Group centred methods. All the methods can be used at higher secondary level for teaching of biology.

Approaches of teaching biology are next in line. In this chapter ten different approaches of teaching biology have been discussed. The approaches have been discussed in a wider perspective, where its application in teaching of science also has been kept in mind. Many illustrations are given to explain the approaches.

Models of teaching, here two models have been discussed, concept attainment model and inquiry training model, followed by approaches. For both the models a few illustrations have been discussed.

The models of teaching are followed by Laboratory. In the chapter on laboratory apart from types and setting of laboratory. An attempt has been made to discuss, pre-lab discussion, post-lab discussion, safety measures, first aid box and assessment of biology practicals.

Curriculum Organization is ninth chapter it covers modern concept of curriculum.

Variables affecting curriculum have been discussed next. It also focuses on characters of curriculum, defects in curriculum, principles, styles of curriculum development and modern trends in biology curriculum.

Teaching Aids is followed by Curriculum organization, wherein audio, visual, audio-visual, aids through activity and many other ways of making biology teaching interesting have been mentioned.

Next and the eleventh chapter focuses on learning biology by doing various activities and its scope in biology textbook has been mentioned. It focuses, on Herbarium, Vivarium, Terarium, field visit, aquarium, museum, garden, science club and science fair.

Last and the final chapter focuses on the evaluation criteria for various programmes that can be adopted to make teaching and learning of biology more interesting. The chapter also highlights the written evaluation, practical evaluation and also criteria for evaluation of various other activities.

Dr. Archana Tomar
Lecturer, Department of Education.
Centre of Advanced Study in Education
Faculty of Education and Psychology.
Maharaja Sayajirao University of Baroda
Baroda

Acknowledgements

Teaching of Biology came up as a demand from the students of biology method group in B. Ed since a couple of years. They constantly said "There is a book on teaching of science, and teaching of all other subjects in the library but we hardly see any book on teaching of biology. They always told me madam why don't you write the book on teaching of biology". So first of all I thank all the biology method students for inspiring me to write a book on Teaching of Biology and for sharing some of their ideas with me during classroom discussions.

My sincere thanks goes to Prof. K. C. Upadhyay, Vice Chancellor of the Maharaja Sayajirao University of Baroda, Vadodara. A Scientist in the field of life sciences for writing the foreword of my book.

I would like to express a deep sense of gratitude to Prof. R. G. Kothari, Head CASE Dean Faculty of Education and Psychology, Maharaja Sayajirao University of Baroda, Vadodara, for all the support provided by him.

I thank Prof. Sneha Joshi, Former Dean, Faculty of Education and Psychology, the Maharaja Sayajirao, University of Baroda, who sincerely went through all my chapters in a limited time and helped me in bringing out some modifications.

I am thankful to Dr. Anjali Khirwadkar and Dr. Chhaya Goel for clarifying my doubts whenever I had some confusion and also inspiring, motivating and supporting me in my endeavour.

I am thankful to my father, mother and brother's who constantly supported me in this endeavour. My acknowledgement will be incomplete if I do not thank my father-in-law who took up many of my responsibilities at the domestic front. I am greatly indebted to my husband Girish and my daughter Muskan for all the tolerance and patience that they have supported me.

Finally I thank the publishers Kalpaz Publications for timely printing the book and bringing it in the market.

Dr. Archana Tomar

1
Nature and Scope of Biology

Introduction

Ever since the origin of the mankind on the planet earth, different kinds of organisms have lived on this planet — they came, they evolved and some of them disa ppeared or became extinct. This phenomenon of new genera of organisms coming on earth and modifying their life patterns has continued for centuries. The most evolved organism on earth is the one who can defend itself from all the changes occurring in the environment, the weak are those who cannot survive the changes successfully. Biology deals with study of life and the living organisms.

Since the beginning of the human civilization human beings have tried to understand the nature around them. This nature comprises of plants and animals. The study of plants and animals, their life and life patterns is the content of biology.

How Biology is at the Base of Every Subject?

Biology deals with plant kingdom and animal kingdom; the most evolved organism in the animal kingdom is the human being. Human beings, the Homo sapiens are the highest evolved organisms on the planet earth. This statement is possible as they have modified, shaped and changed the world according to the needs and requirements. They no longer live the most primitive and natural life lived by any other organism on the earth. They have the best amenities and comforts for themselves because of the function of their brains.

- Early man started staying in caves which were naturally made.
- Then made tree huts, gradually made houses.
- Then settled near the rivers, tired of hunting and searching for food in odd season began sowing seeds and found agriculture.
- Developed their own language for communication, to make certain instruments metals were found.
- For the want of heat; generated it by hitting two stones, invented the potters wheel to make some vessels, later exchanged items through barter system, gradually searched.
- Mathematics to make counting convenient, then made different currencies, they made drawings and arts in the leisure time. Made clothes out of leaves and then by different sticks and cotton.
- To increase the productivity of agriculture fertilizers were researched.
- To control pest, pesticides were found.
- To make instrumentation possible, physics was found.
- To make the living and working in night possible, electricity was found.
- To make cooking possible, gas was found.
- To move from one place to another automobiles were found.
- For faster communication post, telegraph, computer and internet were found.
- To make flying possible, planes and helicopters were invented; the inspiration was taken from birds.
- To sail in water, rafts, boats, ships, submarines, hovercrafts were found. Inspiration was taken from fishes.
- To cure human ailments medicine was found.
- To entertain human beings dance, drama, music, television, videos, CD's etc were found.

- To generate electricity generators were found, dynamos were found.
- To save us from external threats many different types of weapons were made.
- To maintain our own supremacy on earth we have made astronomy.
- We invented education to train the human genera in various disciplines.
- And many more such inventions and discoveries have been possible to make the human life more simple and better.

From the statements stated above one thing is very clear, biology is at the base of any discipline in some or the other way because the inventions and discoveries are done after all for the betterment of living organisms, the living organism is centre to any development on this globe. Biology deals with this crucial matter of dealing with, life, its processes and environment in which the organism lives. If we see the development of human race and try to study any thing and every thing that affects the human being perhaps we may not be able to understand the content, as for each area there is different discipline.

Nature of Biology

The biological sciences occupy an important position in teaching as well as research activities in India. However, like every thing else in this country, there is enormous diversity, not only in the research areas pursued, but also in the pattern and contents of the various teaching programmes.

Biology Teaching: Present Trends

Instruction in Biology/Life Sciences starts at the primary school level when the young children begin to understand the properties of living beings and their diversity. Biology constitutes a significant component of the Science curriculum and is studied by all students till the middle school level. At the secondary school level (9th and 10th standards), Biology becomes a part of science textbook. The process of chanalization starts at the higher secondary level (11th and 12th standards) with a largely (though not absolutely) irreversible selection of future choices. Students who desire to prepare for a career in medical practice usually select biology as one of their subjects at the higher secondary level. In Gujarat there is no such bifurcation of biology and mathematics, so the area of engineering and medicine are both open for the students.

Generally, those unable to enter the medical stream after school opt for admission to the B.Sc. (Bachelor of Sciences, 3 years) programme in biology-related subjects that is offered by almost all the universities in the country, either directly or through their affiliating colleges. At the B.Sc. level, subjects like Botany, Zoology, Microbiology, etc. are most common. Some universities also offer Biochemistry, Physiology, Genetics, Biotechnology, etc. at the B.Sc. level, although in most, these subjects are offered only at the M.Sc. level. Very few places treat Biology or Life Sciences as a whole at the B. Sc. level. In most cases, the students who opt for biology-related subjects at the B.Sc. level cannot study Physics or Mathematics, etc. at the same time, although Chemistry is usually allowed.

The 3-year B. Sc. degree is followed by a 2-year M.Sc. (Master of Science) course, which is an essential pre-requisite for a Ph.D. The Masters programme is generally confined to the major sub-divisions like Botany, Zoology, Microbiology, Physiology, Biochemistry, Genetics, Biotechnology, etc. A limited number of universities also offer M.Sc. in Marine Biology, Aquaculture, Fisheries, Entomology or Biophysics, etc. A few universities offer M. Sc. in "Life Sciences" or "Biological Sciences." In some of these, the student can opt for a greater emphasis on "animal" or "plant" sciences.

Following the M.Sc., students who so desire can undertake research for a Ph.D. degree at a university department or other research institution (the research institutions cannot give their own degree and thus need to be affiliated to a university). Generally, the Ph.D.

involves only research, although several places require a minimal amount of course work in addition to research.

In recent years, a number of universities have initiated integrated programmes for M.Sc. or Ph.D. degrees. The integrated M.Sc. programme (5 years) starts after the higher secondary level and takes the student through to a M.Sc. degree, while the integrated Ph.D. programme (5 years) starts after the student has completed the B.Sc. After two years of course work (equivalent to M.Sc.), the next three years are devoted to Ph.D. research.

The range covers the most commonly available courses in Botany or Zoology at B.Sc. as well as at the M.Sc. levels extends from so-called "classical" botany or zoology to "modern" biology, although considerable variations in emphasis are manifest in the syllabi of different universities. An increasing number of students in recent years have shown preference for "modern" biology and opt to study subjects like Biotechnology, Genetics, Molecular Biology, etc., rather than the traditional Botany or Zoology. The range of laboratory exercises carried out by the students varies vastly but remains limited, in a majority of cases, due to constraints in resources.

It is a general perception that a holistic teaching of biology has suffered in recent years, mostly due to the fact that "Molecular Biology" appears more highly "respected" and attractive for the future career. Furthermore, since the teaching of "classical biology" topics like taxonomy, anatomy, etc. has become increasingly "dry" and restricted to the classroom, fewer students enjoy such subjects (Lakhotia, 1991). Consequently, the quality of research in areas related to basic biology, biodiversity, etc. remains less than satisfactory. Additionally, since the university system in general fails to attract talented "molecular biologists" due to their relatively poor infrastructure, the overall quality of academic manpower has perceptibly declined in the universities, and this is compounded by the fact that fewer of the brighter students now want to go for higher studies in the basic sciences.

Biological research in India: Patterns, Policies and Funding

In addition to the more than 250 regular and "deemed" universities, a large number of autonomous research institutions have been established in India, mostly by governmental agencies like the Council of Scientific and Industrial Research (CSIR), the Departments of Science and Technology (DST), Biotechnology (DBT), Atomic Energy (DAE), etc. Each of these has its own specific research objectives. A number of state governments have also set up research institutes in life science related areas. The CSIR has the largest chain of national laboratories spread across the country, a good number of, which are biology oriented. In recent years, several privately owned research institutions have also come into existence.

With such a large network of universities and research institutions, biological research encompasses a vast range of topics in India. Research in organismic or "classical" biology is largely confined to the university system, while most of the biologically-oriented research institutions place greater emphasis on molecular biology/cell biology and biotechnology-related research. Since research in molecular biology and related fields is more finance-sensitive, the university system generally lags behind in these areas, as compared with the various research institutions, where the laboratories are generally better equipped. In most places, research work is mainly carried out by students pursuing their Ph.D. degree. The culture of post-doctoral research fellows has still to be established.

Most of the universities have little money of their own to support research. The University Grants Commission (UGC) and the Department of Science and Technology (DST) have programmes whereby identified departments in different universities can get additional funding for general development and/or research in specific areas. However, in order to carry out in-depth research, the individual faculty members need to get external funding for research projects. Multiple sources of funding exist. Agencies like DST, DBT, DAE (BRNS), CSIR, UGC, DRDO, etc. all support biological research, basic as well as applied. Although different funding agencies have identified their own thrust areas for priority support (the respective websites listed in Appendix 1 may be visited for details), each of them continues to support a "good" research proposal in almost any area of biology. Thus the Department of Biotechnology (Govt. of India), which was created in the 1980s specifically to promote biotechnology in India, also maintains programmes to support basic molecular biological research. Likewise, the Defence Research & Development Organization (DRDO, Govt. of India) also supports basic as well as applied biological research. Each funding agency has its own peer review system to screen proposals and approve the quantum of funding. Projects are generally supported for three years. In addition to individual projects, several agencies also provide more substantial grants for the establishment of major facilities, etc. Several such "national facilities" (for example, facilities for NMR, DNA and protein sequencing, confocal microscopy, micro-array analysis, etc.) have been created across the country. These facilities have worked with varying degrees of success. Private/industrial support for research is not yet substantial.

Future of Biological Sciences in India: Challenges

Public interest in biology has greatly increased in recent years, thanks to the much discussed developments in genomics and biotechnology. Molecular biology/biotechnology and environmental studies/ecology/biodiversity have attracted the attention not only of policy makers but also of young persons and prospective biologists. India is perhaps one of the few countries that have a separate agency to promote research and applications in biotechnology, in addition to regular teaching programmes in Biotechnology at the undergraduate and Master's levels. Likewise, bioinformatics has been vigorously promoted, and a number of distributed informatics service centres have been set up across the country by the DBT.

While the increased interest in molecular biology/ biotechnology is visible in better quality training, research and other products, progress in the areas of environmental studies/ecology and biodiversity has not been as notable. This is due in part to the fact that good experts in these areas are no longer readily available, because of the general dislike among students, teachers and researchers for taxonomy/morphology and anatomy. As a consequence, a holistic approach to biology is missing.

An incomplete understanding of the biological system also impairs optimal realisation of the benefits of the significantly improved training and research in molecular biology/biotechnology. Biotechnology is currently taught as an independent subject even at the B.Sc. level, unfortunately also in places where neither the teachers nor the laboratories are adequately equipped for the job. Similarly, there is considerable euphoria over the great advances in genomics/ proteomics, etc., but once again, in the absence of a good understanding of biology (especially genetics, cell biology and higher level biological organization), the anticipated "quick" benefits of these technologies have often remained elusive.

As in many other countries, fewer students are now interested in teaching and research as career. Many of those who study biology-related subjects at B.Sc. and M.Sc. levels do so in the hope of entering the biotechnology industry, which is unfortunately still not established in the country. Moreover, given the poorly equipped teachers and laboratory facilities, training of such students is, in many cases, less than satisfactory, and this adds to their frustrations. If this situation continues, the increased interest in biology may wane. To sustain this interest in biology and reap its benefits, there is an urgent need in the country to reorient the teaching programmes in biology. We need a judicious mix of the "classical" and "modern" biology. At the same time it is essential to revamp higher education, specially the university system.

The general lack of interest on the part of the younger generation in a career in science is compounded by the "brain-drain." The relatively good training in molecular biology is encouraging more and more of the brighter younger scientists to "go West." Very few return to the country to undertake productive academic activities. The other type of "brain-drain" occurs within the country itself: away from the university system and toward research institutions and national laboratories. There are a variety of avoidable and unavoidable reasons for this intra-national brain drain that has already resulted in a serious decline in the quality of academia in the university system.

Some efforts have been initiated in recent years at different levels to address the above mentioned factors of limitation. There is an increased awareness of the need for an integrative approach in teaching and research in all areas of biology. With a view to initiate a wider appreciation of a holistic approach to biology, the Indian National Science Academy organised a 2-day seminar on Integrative Biology in March, 2000, with participation by scientists and technologists representing different disciplines (Lakhotia, 2000, 2001). The Indian Institute of Technology (IIT) at Kanpur, a premier institution primarily devoted to engineering and technology, has started a new Department of Biological Sciences and Bio-engineering to promote various realms of biology (and not just biotechnology). Some universities (e.g., the Banaras Hindu University) are planning to initiate new courses in Biology at the undergraduate level so that those studying Physics, Mathematics, etc. can also have the option of studying Biology. The Indian Academy of Sciences, Bangalore, has initiated an ambitious "Project Lifescape," involving a large number of teachers and students at undergraduate and post-graduate levels, to address the challenge of monitoring biodiversity for conservation, sustainable use and control. This project has already resulted in a network of collaborating biology teachers in different parts of the country. With a view to improve the quality of biology teaching across the country, the University Grants Commission (a regulatory body for higher education in the country) has recently proposed new sets of syllabi in different areas of biology for adoption by the universities, with appropriate modifications as locally required. While these are welcome signs, such efforts need to be initiated and sustained on a much wider scale.

The ordinary citizen of today is increasingly aware of the need to maintain the environment and biodiversity, of the potential benefits of biotechnology/ genetic engineering, etc. There is also an increasing awareness about genetic disorders, their diagnosis and possible cure. All these concerns ensure that Biology will continue to be a major discipline for teaching and research in India in the coming decades. However, young teachers and researchers do not generally find the university system attractive enough for their careers. This has a long-term detrimental consequence. The various academic bodies and governmental agencies need to work together to tackle the socio-economic and other factors that are adversely affecting the university system. At the same time, the enthusiasm for molecular biology/biotechnology, considered as the cure-all tool for understanding life and exploiting its properties for betterment of mankind, must not be allowed to undermine the importance of other areas in biology. The rich floral and faunal diversity of the Indian sub-continent remains largely unexplored. This deficiency must be addressed with equal vigour, not only for the sake of knowledge in itself, but because comprehensive knowledge of this biodiversity is bound to provide new insights into evolution, ecology, development, etc. In addition, and perhaps more significant from the currently favoured point of view of business potential: a good knowledge of the flora and fauna is essential for a rational development of the traditional medical systems.

In order to understand what should be the content of biology one must be clear with the objectives of teaching biology. One must appreciate that biology is part of science. Science is of two-type natural science and physical science, physics and chemistry belong to physical sciences where as biology pertains to natural science. In physical science the nature and the structure of an element or instrument does not change just because of its placement in some place. If we see natural science, which emerges from nature, cell is the basic structural and functional unit of any organism. Cell has different shape, size, structure and function depending upon the place where it is located; another difference is the cell capacity of totipotency. The cell has the total potential within it to generate and regenerate; that is, it has the capacity to live and grow and duplicate, which is not possessed by any other components of the physical sciences. Thus, biology is different from other discipline. It has two distinct branches — classical biology and the applied biology. The classical biology deals with classification, nomenclature, evolution that is based on similarities, differences, missing links, connecting links and is also related with the genetic development and origin of life botany, zoology. Whereas applied biology deals with biotechnology, microbiology, biochemistry, genetic engineering, biostatistics, cloning, genome researches, horticulture, apiculture, sericulture, pisciculture, orinthology, environmental studies, forestry, wild life studies, medicine, agriculture, etc.

General Biology & Biomedical Science

The various agencies that support development and training in life sciences are as follows; UNESCO, NSF (National Science Foundation), USAID, Asia-Pacific International Molecular Biology Network, Third World Academy of Sciences (TWAS), Third World Network of Scientific Organizations (TWNSO), Third World

Organization for Women in Science (TWOWS), World Bank, Organization for Economic Co-operation and Development (OECD), NATO Science and Environmental Affairs Division, International Council of Scientific Unions (ICSU), Asia-Pacific Economic Cooperation (APEC), Biotechnology and Biological Sciences Research Council (BBSRC), The Welcome Trust and there are few more from countries like Japan, Germany and Europe. The main funding agencies in India are DBT, DST, CSIR, DAE (TFIR, BARC).

2
Objectives of Biology Teaching

Objectives of Teaching Biology at Secondary and Higher Secondary Level

- Development of awareness of interest and inquisitiveness towards the environment so that the students acquire knowledge of the essential biological facts, concepts, principles, processes terms etc. based on the elementary knowledge of living organisms.
- To make students understand and appreciate the unity and the diversity in the structure, organs, existence and development of living organism and to recognize the relationship between structure and functions.
- To put more stress on the relevant and important aspects like environment conservation, pollution, position of man in biosphere and his impact on it.
- To provide a balanced view of biology so that the student may develop a modern outlook of the subject.
- To enable the student to recognize the social and economic implication of biology and related to the needs of the mankind in the wider sense.
- To develop the skills in observation and experimentation.

- To encourage students creativity, innovation and improvisation.
- To enable the students to carefully assess and interpret simple biological phenomena from daily life.
- To help the students to acquire a working knowledge of the portions of physics, chemistry and mathematics which are necessary for the proper understanding of biology.
- Apart from these the objectives of teaching biology includes careful and close observation.
- To develop scientific attitude, not to believe in blind beliefs, not to jump to conclusion with inadequate data.
- To develop scientific method and scientific temper.
- To develop rational thinking, critical thinking pertaining to various issues affecting life on earth.

Scenario at the School Level

Since the time India got its freedom, i.e, 1947 till date 2003 we have celebrated fifty-six years of independence. In the bygone years we have achieved many milestones in the national scenes in the field of economics, in science and technology. We have achieved the levels of self-sufficiency in many areas. The development goes on to say our education system is strong and healthy plus it is quite viable in the face of global competition. If we have progressed in such an enormous way, it seems we have best of the educators and best of the education available. If we talk about teaching of biology, we have addressed to number of problems facing human life through biology. Biology discusses about the habit and habitat of living organisms on the planet earth. Interrelationships of plants and animals, it talks about their evolution from single cell organisms to complex animals, it deals with their nomenclature, its classification, environmental issues, health issues, issues pertaining to various systems functioning in the organisms and their evolution from one level to another. It focuses on the heredity and hereditary material. It also focuses on issues of socio-economic concern like population control, environment preservation, conservation of natural resources, animal breeding, plant breeding, and economic importance of sericulture, apiculture, etc.

Looking at the content of biology and it being taught over a period of fifty-six years one thing can be said. The school going population have acquired all this knowledge, values and skills necessary and are ready to combat any of the problem pertaining to the content area of biology. They may also be in a position to lend their voice to solve many of the environmental problems facing human generation. They would also have better understanding of the processes and products of biology. They may be aware about the flora and fauna on the planet earth. Perhaps they may be even aware about the life processes and their interdependence. If we have been able to achieve our objectives of teaching biology as a school subject, above mentioned set of behaviours are expected from the clientele of education in today's society. Schools are the places that satisfy the curiosity of students and answer the questions raised by the students. But does this happen? If at all we have achieved the set of objectives stated above, we would definitely see the following.

- A well developed garbage management system, no spiting around.
- Smaller queues at the hospital and doctors clinics.
- A better agricultural crop without the fear of consuming heavy metals.
- Air free of pollution, water pure and potable.
- Fruits and vegetables without pesticides.
- More use of natural things, i.e, bio degradable things.
- Use of recycled products, rather than increasing the garbage pile.
- A more rational life style with lesser stress and burden.

- Good water harvest system and conservation of natural resources.
- And a strong knowledge of fundamentals.

Now, if we see the current scenario we find the opposite we do have awareness of the various problems but we do not have action programmes, it seems we teach them to just inform them and do nothing about it. We do advocate that students should know the structure function relationship but teaching according to teleological approach is seldom done. Topics pertaining to environmental conservation a mere lip say. A research conducted in this area revealed though students prefer walking for short distance in the written questionnaire but in practice used mopeds and other two wheelers for short distances. We have not been able to reach to the implementation stage of many 'so called' "nice recommendations". Students memorize such sweet recommendations and write in examination do not feel necessary to implement in their real life perhaps they feel the content taught in school is far from reality and is meant to just pass examinations. Similarly the concept of balanced diet student may score ten on ten in the written examination but can be very fussy about one's own food habit and may prefer food having low nutrition value. As far as skill development in biology is concerned they are important part of biology learning. We have cancelled animal dissection from biology practicals at school level that does mean we will continue to train them in diagram drawing or diagram photocopying and not observation of important characteristics in the living organisms. Of course creativity is left to computer, internet and library projects. What to say about social biology, biology textbook has chapters on reproduction and family planning which are seldom taught. We can see how each day an Australia is added to India in terms of population. I guess learning of biology has not yielded the expected results perhaps it being taught in isolation, biology cannot be understood without the help of physics, chemistry, mathematics, statistics, language, the integration approach is the answer for solving problems pertaining to biology, say for example, air pollution, the components of air fall in the area of chemistry, water pollution the detergents, pesticides and fertilizers polluting water fall in the area of chemistry, fertilizers used in soil, in structure of DNA pentose sugar phosphate etc, are the elements of chemistry, water, chlorophyll are all pertaining to chemistry. ATP and its composition, active transfer of material in the cell, and many more processes are directly linked with physics. For teaching such points instructional objectives play a vital role.

Instructional Objectives: Instructional objectives are statements written in the future tense the instructional objectives are stated in terms of students performance i.e., the student will be able to... The instructional objectives are of two types the general objectives and the specific objectives.

General Objectives: They are long term, they need longer time in accomplishment. They do not indicate an action verb. The general objectives are broad and based on the subject objectives. For example Students will be able to know the effect of population explosion on environment.

Specific Objectives: The specific objectives are stated in the behavioural terms of the students, they can be manifested, and they can be measured and evaluated. For an objective to be specific one must specify the condition in which the objective will be achieved, the minimum expectation from the students is stated in explicit terms.

Purpose of Instructional Objectives

Instructional objectives communicate the expectations of the teacher from the students after teaching or providing the learning experiences. Consequently, the learning objectives have to be identified on the basis of knowledge, the appropriate depth or detail, and how the students are to use the knowledge. For a traditional 35-minute lecture, usually three to five learning objectives can be constructed. The

Level of Taxonomy	*General Objectives*	*Specific Outcome Action Verbs*
Knowledge	Knows terms Knows specific facts Knows rules Knows classifications and categories Knows criteria Knows methods and procedures Knows principles and generalizations Knows theories and structure	Defines Names States Identifies Describes Distinguishes
Comprehension	Translates communications Interprets relationships Extrapolates from given data	Interprets Converts Explains Predicts Generalizes Infers
Application	Applies principles	Uses Solves Constructs Prepares Demonstrates
Analysis	Analyzes organizations and relationships	Discriminates Outlines Diagrams Differentiates Infers Explains
Synthesis	Produces new arrangements	Designs Organizes Rearranges Compiles Modifies Creates
Evaluation	Judges on the basis of external criteria Judges on the basis of evidence	Appraises Compares Contrasts Discriminates Criticizes Detects

instructional objectives give direction to the teacher to select appropriate learning experiences they also provide a framework for evaluation of the subject matter. Clarity in the objective gives a rationale for selection of appropriate method, media and approach. The objectives are of different types and they are hierarchically arranged one after the other. There are three domains of objectives.

- Cognitive
- Affective
- Psychomotor

One of the most popular classification schemes was the one developed in 1956 by a small group of researcher working with Benjamin Bloom. In 1956, Bloom identified six distinct levels of cognitive understanding, and organized them into a taxonomy of objectives in the cognitive domain. From basic to complex, the taxonomy categories are: Knowledge, Comprehension, Application, Analysis, Synthesis, and Evaluation. The taxonomy levels can be coupled with general objectives, and specific outcome action verbs, which lead to that level. "One of the more frustrating aspects of this taxonomy is its forgotten attribution to the rest of the team. Bloom was the first name listed in alphabetical order of multiple editors, so many that they became the ubiquitous "and others" of a taxonomy that was developed by a committee of people.

One advantage of learning objectives is that you can use them to direct students to material not covered in class.

Tips for Constructing Instructional Objectives

- Objectives should be stated in terms of student behaviour and the level of specificity that is expected
- Objectives should use an action verb that indicates the depth of understanding expected (see table above)
- Objectives should be stated precisely using terms that have uniform meaning and are consistent with their reading resources

- Objectives should be realistic

Categories in the Cognitive Domain

1. *Knowledge:* It is the first and the lowest level of the cognitive domain. At this stage students are merely supposed to recall the information of terminology; specific facts; ways and means of dealing with specifics (conventions, trends and sequences, classifications and categories, criteria, methodology); universals and abstractions in a field (principles and generalizations, theories and structures): Knowledge is (here) defined as the remembering (recalling) of appropriate, previously learned information.
   - Defines; describes; enumerates; identifies; labels; lists; matches; names; reads; records; reproduces; selects; states; views.
   - Student will be able to define the term ecosystem.
   - Student will be able to label the diagram of digestive system.
   - Student will be able to reproduce the structure of DNA etc.

2. *Comprehension:* Grasping (understanding) the meaning of informational materials. The second level of cognitive domain is comprehension. Bloom includes three kinds of intellectual skills in the comprehension level. The first is translation, the ability to make one for one conversion from one language to another. The second skill is interpretation, which is the ability to generalize or paraphrase information. The third is extrapolation, which is the ability to go a little beyond the information given and make predictions reflecting each of these skills.
   - Classifies; cites; converts; describes; discusses; estimates; explains; generalizes; gives examples; makes sense out of; paraphrases; restates (in own words); summarizes; traces; understands.
   - Students will be able to describe the process of photosynthesis

- Students will be able to explain the causes of soil erosion.
- Students will be able to discuss the causes of environmental degradation.

3. *Application*: The third level of the cognitive domain is application. Application is essentially the act of applying some abstraction to a new or unique concrete examples, without prompting. The use of previously learned information in new and concrete situations to solve problems that have single or best answers.

- Acts; administers; articulates; assesses; charts; collects; computes; constructs; contributes; controls; determines; develops; discovers; establishes; extends; implements; includes; informs; instructs; operationalizes; participates; predicts; prepares; preserves; produces; projects; provides; relates; reports; shows; solves; teaches; transfers; uses; utilizes.
- Given the information about terrestial ecosystem and its components, students will be able to relate the components in the desert ecosystem.
- Given the information about preservation of plant as herbarium, the students are able to preserve the plants.

4. *Analysis*: The fourth level of the cognitive domain is analysis. At this level students should be able to break an idea into its constituent elements or internal organizational principles and to perceive relationship among those elements or principles within one "whole", or between several "wholes", Analysis in its fundamental form, is seeing similarities and differences between things. The breaking down of informational materials into their component parts, examining (and trying to understand the organizational structure of such information to develop divergent conclusions by identifying motives or causes, making inferences, and/ or finding evidence to support generalizations.

- Breaks down; correlates; diagrams; differentiates; discriminates; distinguishes; focuses; illustrates; infers; limits; outlines; points out; prioritizes; recognizes; separates; subdivides.
- Students will be able to differentiate between a gymnosperm and angiosperm flower.
- Students will be able to correlate population growth with environmental degradation.
- Students will be able to separate a monocot plant from the given sample.

5. *Synthesis*: The fifth level of the cognitive domain is synthesis means creation of something new from previously existing elements or principles. Creatively or divergently applying prior knowledge and skills to produce a new or original whole.

- adapts; anticipates; categorizes; collaborates; combines; communicates; compares; compiles; composes; contrasts; creates; designs; devises; expresses; facilitates; formulates; generates; incorporates; individualizes; initiates; integrates; intervenes; models; modifies; negotiates; plans; progresses; rearranges; reconstructs; reinforces; reorganizes; revises; structures; substitutes; validates.
- Students will be able to compare the homologous organs of the various organisms.
- Students will be able to compare the embryos of various organisms.

6. *Evaluation*: The last, and highest, level of the cognitive domain is evaluation. Evaluation means the formation of a judgment and substantiation or justification of the judgment by reference to facts, examples or criteria. Evaluation then, means considerably more than simply saying that this is better than that. The judgment must be made simply on the basis of specific criteria. Judging the value of material based on personal values/opinions, resulting in an end

product, with a given purpose, without real right or wrong answers.

- appraises; compares and contrasts; concludes; criticizes; critiques; decides; defends; interprets; judges; justifies; reframes; supports.
- Students will be able to critically study the impact of air pollution on human life.
- Students will be able to support the view that monkeys are not the forefathers of human beings.

Structure of the process dimension of the cognitive domain under the revised Taxonomy of Educational objectives (Adapted from Anderson, Krathwohl, et. al., 2001)

1. Remembering
(a) Recognizing
(b) Recalling
2. Understanding
(a) Interpreting
(b) Exemplifying
(c) Classifying
(d) Summarizing
(e) Inferring
(f) Comparing
(g) Explaining
3. Applying
(a) Executing
(b) Implementing
4. Evaluating
(a) Checking
(b) Critiquing
5. Creating
(a) Generating
(b) Planning
(c) Producing

In the revised taxonomy the process terms have been added in terms of "ing" and also synthesis and evaluation have changed their respective places.

The Affective Domain

The affective domain includes emotions, attitudes, feelings, values, morals. Affective domains hierarchy was given by Krathwohl 1964. The objectives according to Krathwohl, Bloom and Masia, emphasize a feeling tone, an emotion or a degree of acceptance or rejection.

1. Receiving: It refers to a students willingness to attend to a particular phenomenon or stimuli or being sensitive to the stimulus

1. Awareness: Learners are aware of the stimulus.

(a) Willingness: Learner should be ready to receive or accept the available stimulus.

(b) Controlled Attention: Learner is consciously selecting the required stimulus.

This is the lowest level.

2. Responding: Refers to active participation by a student i.e., giving response to the stimulus.

(a) Permission/consent to respond: One consciously permit oneself to respond to a particular stimulus.

(b) Satisfaction in response: The learner feels satisfied with the response which he/she gives to a particular stimulus.

3. Valuing: It depends on the worth or value, a student attaches to a particular object, phenomenon or behaviour. It involves increasing internationalization of the sense of warmth and identification with it. It indicates the individual's motivation and commitments underlying the guiding behaviour.

- Acceptance of value: Accepting many values like honesty, cleanliness, punctuality etc.
- Preference of value of all the values accepted, and prefering some of them (which one feels is readily important).
- Commitment: One tries to internalize the preferred values and shows them in his/her behaviour.

4. Organisation: It is concerned with bringing together different values, resolving conflicts among them and building on an internally consistent value system. Thus, emphasis on an internally consistent value system. Thus, emphasis is on comparing, relating and synthesizing values.

- Conceptualization : To understand meaning of the value in a content or situation.
- Organization of values/ value synthesis: these values are further organized.

5. Characterisation: It is the highest level of affective domain and ultimate goal of education. At this level, the individual has a value system that has controlled his/her behaviour for sufficiently long period of time. The individual develops a characteristic life style.

- Generalized set is a set of things after having organized himself comes to generalization conclusion
- Characterization: After having understood it becomes the character of student.

Bloom's Taxonomy: Psychomotor Domain

Modification of works by Simpson, Gronlund, and others

Descriptors of Major Categories in the Psychomotor Domain Illustrative Verbs for Stating Objectives

1. *Imitation* - early stages in learning a complex skill, overtly, after the individual has indicated a readiness to take a particular type of action. Imitation includes repeating an act that has been demonstrated or explained, and it includes trial and error until an appropriate response is achieved. Imitation - begin, assemble, attempt, carry out, copy, calibrate, construct, dissect, duplicate, follow, mimic, move, practice, proceed, repeat, reproduce, respond, organize, sketch, start, try, volunteer

- Impulsion is a drive, inner push and urge that comes unconsciously.
- Overt repetition; Learning through observing, seeing, unconsciously doing.

2. *Manipulation* – individual continues to practice a particular skill or sequence until it becomes habitual and the action can be performed with some confidence and proficiency. The response is more complex than at the previous level, but the learner still isn't "sure of

him/herself." Manipulation - (same as imitation), acquire, assemble, complete, conduct, do, execute, improve, maintain, make, manipulate, operate, pace, perform, produce, progress, use:

(A) Following direction There is a goal and purpose which is tend to move. When goal is known, then one changes.

(B) Direction: The direction one goes, chooses certain actions to be done in that direction.

(C) Fixation: Fixing it at definite place with choice and purpose. It is a consicious attempt of an individual to fix what is being choosed.

- **Precision** - skill has been attained. Proficiency is indicated by a quick, smooth, accurate performance, requiring a minimum of energy. The overt response is complex and performed without hesitation. Precision - (same as imitation and manipulation), achieve, accomplish, advance, automatize, exceed, excel, master, reach, refine, succeed, surpass, transcend
- Reproduction; Reproducing activity with speed and refinement, already learnt, unconsciously.
- Control: Consciously, precisely imitate someone i.e., learner is able to increase, decrease or modify his her action in response to requirement.

3. *Articulation* - involved an even higher level of precision. The skills are so well developed that the individual can modify movement patterns to fit special requirements or to meet a problem situation. Articulation - adapt, alter, change, excel, rearrange, reorganize, revise, surpass, transcend.

- Sequence: in a well connected way, one is able to do it.
- Harmony refers to the co-ordination of action's right sequence in right proposition of time or at right moment.

4. *Naturalization* - response is automatic. The individual begins to experiment, creating new motor acts or ways of manipulating materials out of

understandings, abilities, and skills developed. One acts "without thinking." Naturalization - arrange, combine, compose, construct, create, design, refine, originate, transcend

Automation: Performance of acts by an individuals without his/her awareness or consciousness or that which happens mechanically

5. *Internalization:* that which happens naturally with conscious mind.

The Psychomotor Domain

Psychomotor objectives are those specific to discreet physical functions, reflex actions and interpretive movements. Traditionally, these types of objectives are concerned with the physically encoding of information, with movement and/or with activities where the gross and fine muscles are used for expressing or interpreting information or concepts. This area also refers to natural, autonomic responses or reflexes.

As stated earlier, to avoid confusion, if the activity is simply something that is physical which supports another area — affective or cognitive — term the objective physical rather than psychomotor. This goes to instructional intent. A primary example of something physical which supports specific cognitive development and skills might be looking through a microscope and identifying and drawing cells. Here the instructional intent of this common scientific activity is not to develop specific skilled proficiency in microscope viewing or in reproducing cells through drawing. The key intent in this activity is that a physical action supports or is a vehicle for cognitive growth and furthering recognition skills. The learner is using the physical action to achieve the cognitive objectives — identify, recognize, and differentiate varied types of cells. If you are using a physical activity to support a cognitive or affective function, simply label it as something physical (labeling the objective as kinesthetic, haptic, or tactile is also acceptable) and avoid the term psychomotor.

The objectives are important in teaching biology not only at the instruction level but also at the content level. The importance of biology can be understood by seeing its application around. It is for these values that biology finds its place in school curriculum.

1. Intellectual Value: The great value of Biology is that it helps man to understand life and its forms. It enables one to think to how life must has emerged on earth and diversified into its various forms, shapes and sizes that we see around us. The main aim of biology is "acquisition of knowledge and ideas". The study of biology helps man to study him and his surrounding. What are the components of the ecosystem and their interrelationship?

For eample one is able to know many facts about oneself. How children look like their parents? Which are the factors responsible for heredity? Why people look different? One can know about so many diseases and using once intelligence one can safe guard against the hazards. Thus, biology helps in thinking scientifically and critically.

2. Utilitarian Value: From cradle to grave all the activities of human life are for its betterment. And biology contributes towards it. The food that we eat, the cloths that we wear, houses that we live in, fossil fuel that we use. The medicines that we take are contribution of biology. We have developed better hybrids; we have artificial limb and organ transplants. The green revolution and the flood revolution have made life longer on planet earth.

Biology can also be devastating in the war conditions. It could be used as warfare material to bring mass destruction.

3. Vocational Value: Biology forms the basis of so many studies, which are purely vocational in nature. For example it offers courses like medicine, agriculture, pathology, biotechnology, genetics, microbiologist, paramedicine, sericulture, horticulture, forest and environment, fishery, entomology, animal breeding, plant breeding, musicology etc. It depends on the choice of individual to study a subject in its depth. It also provides activities for leisure time creating, aquarium, vivarium, terrarium, gardening, collection of corals, sponges preservation of plants and animals etc.

4. *Moral Value:* Biology as a discipline tries to seek truth about the nature and reports the same. The facts are proven on the basis of experiments, which can be duplicated and replicated, in a given condition. It works on moral standards.

5. *Aesthetic Value:* The natural beauty that we see around us is joy forever. The nature manifests itself so beautifully; everywhere we see many forms of life so colourful and picturesque. In different fields of biology all the great advances have come from the desire to unveil what Einstein calls "The pre-established harmony".

6. *Psychological Value:* The principal of activity is the main basis of the teaching of biology and satisfies the instincts of curiosity, creativeness, self-assertion, and expression etc. of the students.

So, its quite clear from the above discourse that a subject, which is so valuable and psychologically based so closely connected with our daily life is justified to be included in the curriculum.

7. *Training in Scientific Method*: The study of biology trains the students in attacking the problem according to a certain definite and distinct procedures which is called scientific method. This training can be applied to solve other problems arising in new situation. Following are the steps involved in it.

1. Identifying the problem.
2. Defining the problem.
3. Stating the hypothesis.
4. Collecting data.
5. Setting the experiment to test its validity.
6. Interpreting the data.
7. Drawing conclusion.
8. Generalizing.
9. Applying in new situation.

8. Develop Scientific Attitude: The attitude of a biologist involves critical thinking, observation, open-mindedness, suspended judgment free from superstition etc. The attitude once developed in the students proves useful in all the human activity.

Thus, in short, its inclusion in curriculum should be there because of following points.

1. It helps us to understand ourselves better. Many questions may have occurred about oneself and the world it tries to answer those questions. To seek answers one has to have background and understanding of biology.
2. It helps us to meet the needs by resources available to him i.e., knowledge of crops, domestic animals, medicine, microbiology, and protection from disease, and improvement in quality of life.
3. Solving problem is an important aspect of biology. Example for finding out solution for eradicating small pox, zoologists, microbiologists, medicos, chemist drug manufacturers others pooled their knowledge for combating the disease on a global scale.

   This explains how discoveries require the collaboration of people from other disciplines.
4. It teaches that we are small part of this living planet and we have the responsibility to protect and respect all living organisms.
5. It makes us aware of the intricate relationships that exist among organism in an ecosystem and we should be cautious when we interfere with them.
6. It warns us about the possible environmental hazards caused by our activities like degradation, pollution etc.
7. The study of nature for its own sake is rewarding experience. A biologist can observe enormous diversity of living things. Nature presents us with beauty at its best. Which is depicted by poets and artists at all times. This makes our appreciation of the beauty deeper and richer.

8. It teaches us how science is practiced. How to ask questions and through a process. Process of reasoning and experimenting find answers for them.

3
Biology and Correlation

Correlation means reciprocal relationship between various subjects of the curriculum. The child is interested to learn the things, which are related to his experiences. They can't learn various subjects in isolation while teaching biology the teacher can't ill afford to confine himself to his/her subject alone. If he/she does then how can one expect the children to appreciate and understand all about one branch of biology in isolation from others. So, the correlation of different subjects is very essential for checking artificiality of treatment and for achieving unity of knowledge. It makes learning more easier, interesting and natural.

In basic scheme of education correlation occupies the pivotal position. Here emphasis is laid not only on the correlation of one subject with another but of education with life. The principle of correlation demands that various subjects when taught to a child then they must help him to understand his environment better and carryout his activities in a smooth way.

In order to study correlation of biology with others following divisions can be made.

1. With some discipline of biology.
2. With science subjects.
3. With other school subjects.
4. With physical and social environment.

1. **With some Discipline of Biology**

(a) Biology and Anthropology: As biology is study of living things, Anthropology is study of man and mankind

including the study of the physical and mental constitution of man his cultural development etc. in present and past. For example if teacher is teaching about evolution of human race, one must have adequate knowledge of Anthropology without which he can't justify the treatment of the topic.

(b) Biology with Pathology: While teaching about various diseases and their causes one needs to know biology and its pathological symptoms.

(c) With Genetic Engineering: While teaching about heredity he can talk about genetic manipulation to produce an organism with new combination of inherited properties. He can quote examples of hybrid varieties of rice, wheat etc.

There are many disciplines of biology like medicine, biochemistry, biophysics, microbiology, food technology. Forensic science is correlated with biology etc. that in turn is correlated with each other and other disciplines.

2. With Science Subjects

All the branches of science are interdependent on each other and there are number of facts and principles which are common to various science subjects.

(a) With Chemistry: A teacher while teaching about digestive system should have adequate knowledge of chemistry. He can correlate it with chemistry of different digestive juices and the process of assimilation etc. A good teacher will also tell about food produced in plants. This will help the students to know about formation of some important constituents of diet and their properties and will help him to have a clear picture of digestion.

(b) With Physics: Similarly, biology is related to physics also. There are various instruments which are used in biology like microscope, spectrophotometer, centrifuge etc. All these instruments are the contribution of physics which help in the study of biology. The units of measurement are also the contribution of physics

which are useful in the study of biology. The physics students also study biology of eye and ear.

3. Correlation of Biology with other School Subjects:

Biology is such a subject it can be correlated with any other school subject.

(a) With Language: - Any subject for communication of its thoughts and ideas requires language. Language makes the thought clear, concise, and correct. Thus, biology and language are correlated. Teacher should take up a joint responsibility. For the cultivation of good style in writing essay type answers. The language teacher can ask students to write an essay on diseases etc. He can also give biographies of scientists so that the students are inspired by the discovery.

(b) With Mathematics: There are some topics in biology example graphs, equations, probabilities etc for e.g. while teaching environmental degradation teacher can tell about the statistical analysis of the degradation recorded two years back and can differentiate it with today. This will help the students to know how fast/ slow the degradation is occurring.

(c) With Geography: Geography and biology are very much correlated with each other. The study about soil, climate, distribution of plants and animals, etc, brings the subjects closer to each other effect on climatic factors on plants and animals, the distribution of plants and animals are common in both subjects.

(d) With Craft: This correlation is possible to a greater extent. As students can do wood work, cardboard modeling, clayware students can prepare models of biology like DNA, structure of flower, brain, working model of heart etc. It helps in producing those qualities of thought, application and skill, which are required for the future.

(e) With Fine Arts: Drawing is of immense importance especially in biology. The preparation of charts, and pictures requires some skill in painting. Thus, it is important that the students should be given training in drawing and painting.

(f) With Social and Physical Environment: Biology has changed the whole pattern of society and has affected the social as well as physical environment. One should relate the students by quoting example from daily life of students. S/he should take students to excursion while dealing with the concerned topic. This helps the students to relate their environment with biology.

4
Instructional Planning

For effective organization of any activity planning is required as it gives vision, direction to activity. So let us see what is planning?

Planning is a process of pre-determined, co-ordinate and long-term effort to bring about change in the behavior of students by appropriate allocation of all the resources needed to accomplish definite objectives in order of priority.

Planning is not done in air. In order to plan we need various resources.

Resources: Planning would need physical resources, infrastructure, materials, and books, aids etc. Financial resources to arrange for field trips etc. Human resources the teachers and the taught. Time is another important resource we have just one year to complete the course in 11th standard there are 21 chapters and in 12th standard biology textbook there are 40 chapters. Proper time allocation needs to be done in order to complete the course.

All the resources are to be used judiciously in order to obtain the goals and objectives of the course. For planning one needs to analyze the content properly.

Content Analysis: Content analysis is breaking down the content into the simplest form the smallest content is identified and its relationship with other similar or different topics needs to be established.

For example,

Content analysis of Evidences of Evolution

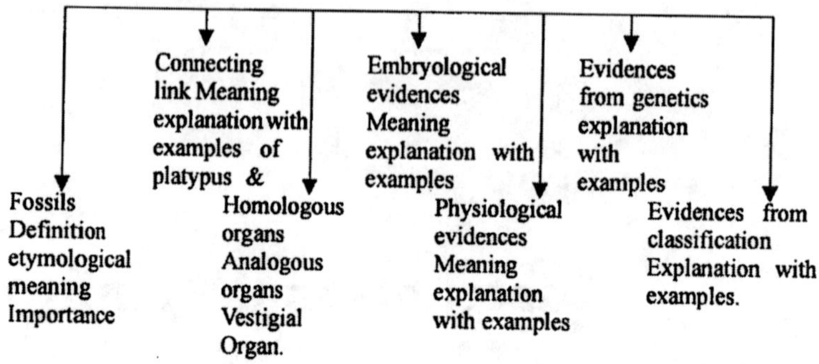

After the analysis of content and its arrangement from simple of complex. Next logical step is to prepare plan.

Importance of Planning

(1) It gives direction to the teacher.
(2) It helps the teacher to prepare in advance.
(3) Teacher can focus on different levels of objectives.
(4) Entire textbook is nicely studied by the teacher so that adequate importance is given to every content area.
(5) Teacher can select appropriate method teaching aids and demonstration and save his/her time.
(6) Makes work systematic and impressionable. Teacher functions in an organized manner.
(7) In absence of planning there is chaos, confusion, no direction, no target, no purpose, wastage of resources, duplication of efforts, wastage of energy.
(8) It helps in gaining confidence, connectivity, continuity, and co-operation from students, co-ordination of various activities and demonstration is possible.

Types of Plans

Based on the duration of planning, the plans can be classified into three types.

Annual Plan	-	Yearly
Unit Plan	-	Monthly
Lesson Plan	-	Daily.

Annual Planning

It is a plan for one full academic year. According to the Gujarat government rules a teacher has to remain on the school campus for 30 hours a teacher is expected to teach for 21 hours in a week 28(2). The school has to function for 240 days in a year out of which 190 day's should be full days. In any circumstances the holidays should not be for more than 80 days out of the 240 days. The 240 Sundays and half days are not included in the 80 days holiday. In a week 27 hours of teaching is carried out for various subjects. Three hours are distributed in recess, assembly cocurricular activities.

In order to cover the courses in the stipulated time one must plan the course for whole year. For an annual plan one requires calendar. Here calendar is the activity calendar prepared for one complete year, which depicts curricular and co-curricular activities along with schedule for term end and final examination. Another thing required is list of holidays, school timetable. Finally, one needs the textbook of Biology.

After scrutinizing the textbook carefully one has to organize the content into units and lesson. Formation of unit makes understanding simple and convenient. The sequence becomes logical and flows smoothly.

A teacher is supposed to teach for 25 to 28 periods. For a biology teacher there are 5 periods of theory each in 11th standard and 12th standard. For practical purpose 3 periods are allotted both in 11th and 12th standard.

Keeping the school calendar in mind, the school timetable and various other activities, the teacher is supposed to organize the content in the annual plan format. One must study the chapter to find out number of period required to complete the chapter.

Annual Plan Format

Sr. No.	Month	Chapter	Periods	Practical	Remarks
1.	June.	Introduction and scope of biology to	2	Introduction to laboratory	
2.	June.	Cell Cell structure, cell division.	3 4 2		
3.	July.	Organism and energy Taxonomy of plants. Classification of Animals	3 3 5		
4.	August.	Virus and Bacteria. Revision	2 4		
5.		Test.			
6.	September.	Body Organization	4		
7.	September.	Origin of life	3		
8.	September.	Evidences of Evolution.	3		
9.	September.	Darwin's theory.	3		
10.	October.	Diwali Vacation.			
11.	November.	Heredity. Hereditary Material Speciation.	5 5 4		
12.	December.	Living organism and Environment population growth and its control. Revision.	4 4 4		
13.	January.	Test. Sports week fun fair picnic preparation for 26th January.			
14.	February.	Plant Breeding. Animal Breeding.	4 5		

15.	March.	Presentation of various projects and Assignment	15		
16.	April.	Teaching Content from 12th and Revision of 11th standard.			

The programme given above is suggestive. The practicals' may go hand in hand with the theory. A list of various teaching aids required for various chapters can also be attached. Also a list of project and assignment to be given in the vacation can also be listed along with the annual plan. If term papers or book reviews are to be given then its list can also be attached along with the annual plan. The annual plan acts as a torchbearer throughout the year. A teacher can know how much course has to be completed. The principal will also know from the annual plan. How much is covered and how much needs to be covered. Similarly annual plan can be prepared for 12th standard.

Advantages of annual planning

1. It helps in organizing the content systematically throughout the academic year.
2. Due to annual planning it is possible to allot adequate time to each content area depending on its importance and complexity.
3. It helps in planning and preparation of various audio visual aids to teach the content plus proper arrangement of demonstration is possible.
4. It helps in conducting various activities evaluation and also has scope for revision.
5. Co-ordination of various teaching learning activities is possible.
6. It removes the element of duplication if more than one teacher is involved in teaching.

While preparing annual plan we classified the chapters according to units. Now let us understand what is a Unit Plan? Before studying unit planning let us study about unit.

What is a Unit?

1. According to Preston: "A unit is as large a block of related subject matter as can be over viewed by the learner".

Samford says that a unit is an "outline of carefully selected subject matter which has been isolated because of its relationship to pupil's needs and interests".

A unit could be combination of three chapters or one chapter. But essential fact is it presents a composite idea or theme. Thematically, it should look like one single, wholesome understandable big chapter, which for convenience has been divided into sub units. It usually has a unit test at the end accompanied with references. Its duration is shorter than that of an annual plan and longer than daily plan.

What is a Unit Plan?

A unit plan is a compilation of precise instructional objectives, related with content, which can be achieved through instructional experiences, with the help of suitable teaching aids. The plan often begins with a rationale and ends with an evaluation instrument. A unit plan represents the teacher's most complete conceptualization of what students will accomplish in a given block of time (usually from 3 to 6 weeks). How they will go about working to ensure success of a unit plan is a teacher's plan of action and his or her overall strategy.

Once the major objectives are written it becomes useful to write subsequent objectives. It facilitates daily lesson planning by breaking the major objectives.

Rational: Must reflect the importance of the skills and content to be learned.

"Why do we learn this?"

Relevance of content

Specifying Content: - A teacher may refer numerous things to specify the content.

- Textbook } Self-confidence
- Library — This will Preparation
- Personal experience — enhance
- Notes — Teacher will be familiar with 'big picture.
- Resource books

Anecdotes - Supplementary information, website, newspaper, T.V., internet.

Technology aids: - charts, models, filmstrips, real material slides transparency, permanent slides on computer (its listing, storage availability address)

Selecting Instructional Experiences

The objectives must suggest appropriate instructional experiences.

Since the objectives, subject matter, materials and instructional experiences have already been selected the writing of lesson plan is facilitated.

Deciding Optional Activities

Teachers may involve students in the activities they are interested in.

Example bulletin board,
model
diorama
panel discussion.
independent project.

2nd by activities designed for exceptional students teacher can prepare bibliography cards slower student can be given material written at a lower level so that they do not fall behind, while brighter students can be directed to more challenging material.

Special reading
Reports
Interviews.

These activities can be tried on experimental basis.

Planning for Evaluation

The final step in unit planning is to construct the instruments needed to determine whether the objective is achieved or not. According to the objectives and the expected levels of skills and competencies the teacher constructs the unit tests prepared with the answer key.

A teacher prepares a Question Bank, which is set of all the possible questions of different types and levels. These questions are

Essay type
Short answer
True or false
Match A with B.
Fill in the blank
Multiple choices
Select type
Supply type
Drawing labeling etc.

They belong to different level.

Knowledge
Understanding
Application
Analysis
Synthesis
Evaluation,

From the Question Bank required questions are selected for the unit test.

Thus, a unit plan is a compilation of precise instructional objectives, subject matter, instructional materials and experiences, optional experiences, and appropriate evaluation instruments, all of which are concerned with a central theme or topic.

A major advantage to unit planning is that such planning usually takes place when teachers have the time and the energy to construct realistic and taxonomically balanced objectives; to sift through a large amount of subject matter and extract that which is most appropriate; to plan varied instructional experiences; to build optional experiences and to build appropriate evaluation instruments.

Unit Plan Components

I Title Page:

(A) Title of the unit.

(B) Name of the course for which unit was designed.

(C) Academic and grade level of students for which the unit was designed.

(D) Brief overview of the unit.

(E) Statement describing preceding and/or following the unit(s).

II Objectives:

(A) Should be stated in observable terms and measurable outcomes.

(B) Should be balanced so that there is not too much emphasis on any particular level (although there should be more higher level cognitive objectives than any other kind)

III Subject Matter

(A) Should contain all the information (facts, definitions, examples, explanations, anecdotes, etc.) Students will need to achieve the objectives.

(B) Should be gleaned from a variety of sources.

IV Materials and Activities

(A) Should include appropriate ordering information for mediated instructional aids.

(B) May be organized as a general outline, as separate lesson plans, or in broad categories such as introduction, development and conclusion.

(C) Should contain an annotated bibliography of sources (both used and possible).

V Optional Activities

(A) Should contain optional and enrichment activities open to all students. With another section designed for exceptional students.

(B) Can serve as a proving ground for innovative ideas.

VI Evaluation Instruments

(A) Must reflect objectives.

(B) Must have answer keys, and or modes, and or checklists.

(C) Greater utilization of evaluation forms other than formal paper and pencil tests recommended.

Lesson Plan

Lesson plan is a plan, which is made for one period of 35 to 40 minutes. It is the daily requirement of a teacher. In this plan the teacher depending upon the content analysis organizes the information systematically for transaction in one period. A Herbatian lesson plan is given here as a sample. It starts with initial information that is the name of teacher, name of school, standard, period and date on which the lesson is to be transacted. Followed by the initial details the entry behavior are written

Initial Details
Entry Behavior
General objectives
Method, media, approach
Introduction
Presentation Stage
(A) teaching points
(B) specific objectives
(C) teacher's activity/learning experience
(D) student's expected activity
(E) point wise evaluation
Recapitulation
Home assignment
Blackboard Summary

Name of the teacher trainee : ABC
Name of the School : XYZ
Subject : Biology
Standard : XI
Period : N

Topic : comparative anatomy

(I) Entry behaviour:

- Students know the meaning of the term 'anatomy'.
- Students know about anatomy of various organisms.
- Students know about vestigial organs.

(II) General objectives:

- Students will be able to understand the concept of vestigial organs.
- Students will know about homologous organs.
- Students will be able to understand concept of analogous organs.

(III) **Method** : Lecture cum discussion
Media : Roll up board
Approach : Inductodeductive

(IV) Introduction:

Good morning class. Yesterday we talked about fossils as one of the evidence of evolution. Today another evidence of evolution, we shall study comparative anatomy of the body of vertebrates gives us an idea about great relationship between comparative anatomy of vertebrates different groups of vertebrates.

(V) Presentation

Teaching. Points	*Specific objectives*	*Teacher activity*	*Student activity*	*Evaluation*
Homologous organs.	Students will be able to define homologous organs.	Teacher: - There are some organs present in different groups of vertebrates which posses common origin, similar structure but different	Students write down the definition of analogous organs.	What are homologous organs?

contd...

		appearance and different functions.		
	Students will be able to give examples of homologous organs.	The fore limps of frog, reptiles, bird, whale, man when compared showed great resemblance in their basic plan structure arrangement of bones very much common they have a common origin. This shows relation ship between different groups of vertebrates of course depending upon habit and habitat they have different function and different appearance so these organs are example of homologous organs.	Students listen carefully.	Which are the examples of homologous organs?
Analogous organs	Students will be able to define analogous organs.	Teacher: there are some organs present in various organisms which are similar in function and appearance but having different origin and different structure.	Students write down the definition of analogous organs.	What are analogous organs? Which are the examples of analogous organs?
	Students will be able to give examples of analogous organs	When wings of various organism such as wings of birds, wings of bat, wings of pterodactyl, wings of insects are compared they show similar function and appearance. These wings have different origin. These wings have different structure too.	Students listen carefully.	
Vestigial organs	Students will take down the definition of vestigial organs.	Teacher: - There are some organs found in some plants and animals that are of no use to the organism although they were useful to the ancestors. These organs are called vestigial organs.	Students will take down the definition of vestigial organs.	What are vestigial organs? Which are the vestigial organs of human body?

		Initially these organs are very useful and well developed in ancestors but are not used over the generations hence in present generation they become useless and non functional and reduced sized these organs are called vestigial organs.		Which is the vestigial organ of python? Which is the vestigial organ of whale?
		Teacher: - which are some of the vestigial organs in human body? Teacher: - Exactly these are some vestigial organs.	Students: - Wisdom tooth, muscles for movement of pinna, appendix etc.	
		Teacher: - Which are the other examples of vestigial organs? Teacher: - Yes any other example. Yes these are the different examples of vestigial organs.	Students: - hind limb bones in skeleton of python. Students: - femur bone in Skeleton of whale.	

(VI) Recapitulation: -

- What are the homologous organs?
- Give examples of homologous organs.
- Give an example of analogous organs.
- Give at least two examples of vestigial organs.

(VII) Home assignment: -

- Draw the diagrams of homologous organs.

dt. Subject Biology class XI

Topic:- Comparative Anatomy

Picture of Vestigial organs 1.

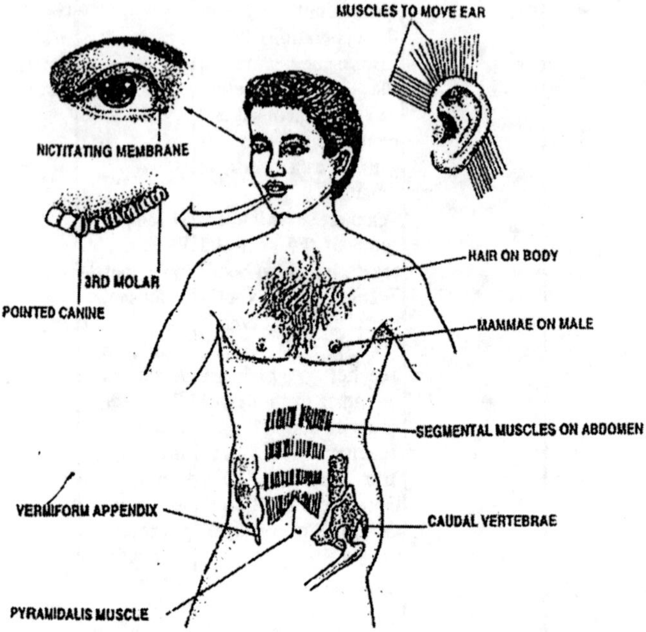

VESTIGIAL ORGANS OF THE HUMAN BODY

(VIII) Reference for teacher:

1. Textbook of science (VIIIth std)
   - Gujarat board.
2. Textbook of Biology (XIth std)
   - Gujarat board.

(IX) Reference for students:

1. Textbook of science (VIIIth std)
   - Gujarat board.

Unit test

(It is discussed in the unit on evaluation)

UNIT PLAN

Sr. No.	Sub-units	No. of Lessons	Time required	Scope of Sub unit	Procedure	Teaching aid
1.	Natural resources Definition amd classfication.	1	35	This Sub Unit gives an idea about natural resources their examples and classfication of natural resources	• Lecture-cum-discussion • Inducto-deductive approach	–
2.	Renewable natural resources and nitrogen cycle.	1	35	This sub-unit deals with different renewable natural resources; their classfication, their examples. Air as a natural resource, and nitrogen cycle.	• Lecture-cum-discussion • Inducto-deductive approach	chart
3.	Water as a natural resource	1	35	This sub-unit deals with water as a natural resources. Types of water available on earth, conservation of water	• Lecture-cum-discussion • Inducto-deductive approach	Flow chart
4.	Soil as a natural resource.	1	35	This sub-unit explains importance of soil as a natural source and need to conserve it and how to do so?	• Lecture-cum-discussion • Inducto-deductive approach	Chart

(contd.)

(contd.)

5.	Forest as a natural resource	1	35	This sub-unit gives us the importance of forces for nature balance and need to conserve it.	• Lecture-cum-discu-ssion • Inducto-deductive approach.	
6.	Non renewable resources	1	35	This sub-unit gives idea about different non-renewable resource and need to conserve them.	• Lecture-cum-discu-ssion • Inducto-deductive approach	
7.	Pollution and war	1	35	This sub-unit gives idea about man made calamities such as war, pollution etc. now they disturb natural balance.	• Lecture-cum-discu-ssion • Inducto-deductive approach	

5
Methods of Teaching

In the schools our goal is to teach the group of students. The group of students is a unique one as they have more or less similar ability; they have assembled for a similar purpose that is learning. These students have individual needs, abilities shared concerns, and they work as a cohesive unit. The students interact with each other with the teacher and the available material in a-pre decided and a set manner so that some changes can be brought about in their behaviour. The changes brought in the behaviour are attributed to the forces of learning. The learning is enforced by the various activities that are carried out by the teacher in the classroom. All the methods have specific steps to be carried out by students and teachers in the form of various learning experiences. These learning experiences vary from method to method. The basic purpose of the method is to simplify and clarify the content for the student based on dominance and passivity the methods are divided into three types.

(1) Teacher centred.
(2) Pupil centred.
(3) Group centred.

Teacher centred methods are those where the teacher is dominating and students are simply passive.

In student centred method the students are active they individually get a chance to do something.

Group centred activities or methods are those methods where the groups are dominant and not the individuals.

Example of Teacher Centered method
(1) Lecture
(2) Historical
(3) Lecture cum demonstration
Example of Student Centered method
(1) Assignments
(2) Laboratory
(3) Heuristic
Example of Group Centered
(1) Project
(2) Discussion

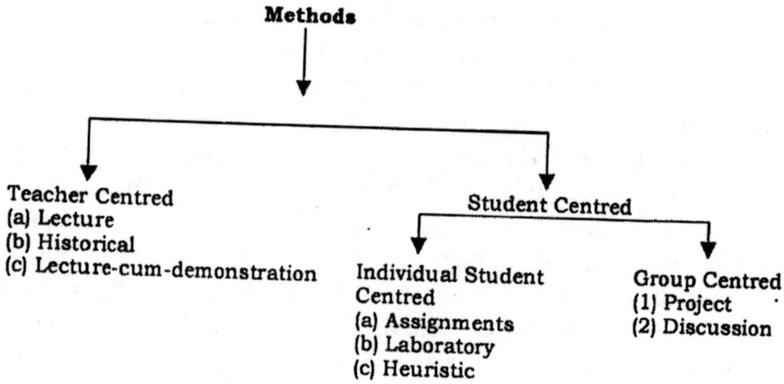

Learning is a change in behaviour and in the cognitive structure of individual as a result of his/her informal interaction with the environment, event, situation, and circumstances or in a formal teaching process. Teaching is a process of achieving prespecified goals in the controlled environment to result into desirable changes in the individual. The environment would consist of various learning experiences provided to reach the desirable objectives. Environment has congenial and facilitative influence on an individual to help him/her change.

The instructional environment can be teacher controlled or learner controlled.

Difference between teacher controlled and learner controlled method

Teacher Controlled	*Pupil Controlled*
(1) Teacher is active in transacting the curriculum students are passive listeners.	Students are active in performing activities and participating in discussion
(2) Extensive laboratory work is not required. As teacher can manage with demonstration.	It requires laboratory as the students have to do individual work.
(3) Emphasis on accumulation of facts and information.	Emphasis is on development of skills, abilities and competencies.
(4) It is economical, as it requires very less infrastructure.	It is expensive as lot of infrastructural facilities is required.
(5) There is no scope for learning by doing or learning by living.	Learning by doing is possible; learning by living is also possible.
(6) Emphasizes repetition and memorization.	Emphasizes on discovery and exploration.
(7) Environment is teacher dominated and authoritarian.	Democratic, participative and involves group decision-making.
(8) Environment is restrictive.	Self-governing environment.
(9) Seating arrangement in rows and columns.	Seating arrangement flexible, mobile.
(10) Retention is lesser as students are passive listeners.	Retention is for a longer time as it is based on principle of learning by doing.
(11) All students are supposed to learn at same pace.	Different students gifted average and slow can learn at their own pace.
(12) Individual student evaluation can be done easily.	Evaluation of students in a group work is very difficult.

LECTURE METHOD

Lecture method is also called as expository method or narration method. It is oral exposition of linked facts, which are woven into a fabric. It is a teacher dominated activity, where teacher takes for 85 per cent of the time in the remaining 15 per cent time, 10 per cent is for question and answer doubt clarification, 5 per cent is silence. Here the role of the students is that of passive listeners. In the Indian context this is the most predominant method where the resources are meager and the library and laboratory facilities are grossly inadequate. It is a unique method, which covers a large chunk of information in small time.

Importance of Lecture Method

Lecture method does not require an elaborate laboratory or a huge library. It only needs a teacher with good oratory skills and powerful content communication of teacher has to be good for its effectiveness. As it requires a patience in listening. The students need to have the ability of note taking. This method is able to cover a large portion of content in small time. Only the teacher requires references. The teacher can enrich and illustrate the content in the class. Through this method we are able to reach many students in a small duration. It is highly economic.

Steps Involved in a lecture method

Step 1. Planning

- Gathering information from various sources, i.e. referring journals, magazines, textbooks NCERT, CBSE etc. even Internet, classifying based on what is required.
- Sequencing the available knowledge based on students understanding, age, ability.
- Sequence it in such a way that it becomes meaningful or understandable.
- Divide it properly into topics and subtopics.

Step 2. Presentation: The presentation is further divided into Introduction, body – teaching aids, Evaluation, conclusion, summary.

Pre-requisite

Students must be made ready to learn

- Student's interest and curiosity needs to be maintained.
- Voice should be loud and clear.
- Too much of movement or too much of monotony must be avoided.
- Blackboard summary should be prepared.
- Teaching aids should be used to clarify complex topics.
- The teaching style should not be authoritarian.
- Students should have a chance to ask question /doubts/clarification.
- The classroom should be properly managed.
- Voice modulation should be practiced to avoid monotony.
- Relevant illustrations should be used for teaching various subjects.
- Time should be given for writing down salient points in their notebook.
- Important points must be stressed again and again.
- Teacher must check speed from time to time. Speed should neither be fast nor slow.
- Continuous evaluation should be practiced while lecturing so that we know our students are with us.
- We must remember that the concentration span of students is of 15 minutes. So after 15 minutes some variation should be there in style or pattern or stimulus.

When to Use Lecture Method?

(1) When the topic is new.
(2) When the content is narrative.
(3) When the content is difficult to comprehend.

(4) When the content is factual.
(5) When the content is informative.

Merits of the Lecture Method

(1) It is highly economical.
(2) It is helpful when the information is factual and given for first time.
(3) It is time saving. A large portion can be covered in short time.
(4) It does not require a library or a laboratory.
(5) With minimum resources it caters to maximum number of people.
(6) It helps in maintaining logical continuity of the content.
(7) It simplifies the task of teacher, as no laboratory work is required.
(8) Effective lectures impress the students to take up the profession.

Demerits

(1) It is not based on the maxim learning by doing.
(2) It becomes boring and monotonous if teacher is not effective.
(3) All content cannot be taught by lecture method.
(4) It does not cater to the individual differences.
(5) It does not help in skill development.
(6) Students hardly get a chance to clarify their doubts, as the communication is one way.
(7) It emphasises rote memorization.
(8) Students do not develop higher thinking abilities rather they are just receptors of knowledge.

How to Improve Lecture Method?

(1) To work on voice: Clarity of speech, proper pronunciation, and proper intonation. Good articulation.
(2) Mastery on language: Along with mastery of content one must also have mastery on language.

(3) Use of Illustrations: One must be able to use stories, illustrations anecdotes even light humor to make classes interesting

(4) Teaching Aids: Making use of various audio visual aids in learning not just clarifies the complex content it also gives a break in the form of shift in stimulus.

(5) Question Answers: Evaluation is important at both the junctions i.e., formative as well as summative. The formative could be step by step after teaching few points. And summative could be after teaching the entire content. Question answers in between the class help to maintain student's interest in the content. It also keeps students attention on toes that any one can be asked.

(6) Gestures can be used to illustrate the content. While introducing new & abstract concepts.

Where lecture method can be used?

- Gene and gene Action
- Genetics
- Evolution
- Evidences of evolution
- Classification of plants and animals
- Topics pertaining to history, Discovery
- Hereditary material
- Plant breeding etc.

HISTORICAL METHOD

Historical method is also a teacher-dominated method where the teacher is actively involved and the pupils are passive listeners the name itself suggests that historical method deals with the history or the evolution of topic from a simple one to a complex. This method can be used at any stage to develop curiosity and interest in the subject. The scientists for ages have sacrificed their lives to give us the comforts that we enjoy today. As teacher it is our earnest responsibility that we bring before the students the pleasures and pains of the scientists who are glorified in the textbooks for 'Ages'. Students must know the hard work and sacrifices that are made to become so famous. The values of hard work and persistence, the value of courage and conviction, the fire to find something inspired the discoveries they made can be learnt through this method.

Historical method gives an explanation or a historical account of the scientist and his/her inventions. It also gives chronological events of the happenings. It is similar to story telling. The student finds this method to be very interesting as they get to learn the process and the developmental stages of our inquiry or investigation. History or background information of a topic needs to be given. It arouses the interest of students.

Merits

(1) It helps in understanding the contribution of scientist.
(2) It helps in increasing interest and curiosity.
(3) It gives a brief view of the life of the scientist.
(4) It helps to sequence things chronologically.
(5) It motivates students to learn values from the life of scientist.
(6) It has all merits of lecture method.

Demerits

(1) It may not be applicable for all types of contents.
(2) Everything cannot be taught by this method.
(3) Teacher dominates it so it can be monotonous and boring.
(4) It is not based on learning by doing.
(5) It has all the demerits of a lecture method.

Topics that can be taught through this method.

- Origin of life
- Evolution
- Cell theory
- Mendelian law
- Different types of classification, etc.

LECTURE CUM DEMONSTRATION METHOD

Definition

Demonstration is a planned manipulation of equipments and materials by a teacher to the end that students observe all or some of the manifestations of one or more scientific principles. Piper and Catman in 1970

Importance of Demonstration:

- Science is experimental in nature hence by this method one is able to learn by seeing the experiments.
- It helps to proceed from concrete to abstract. The experiments are replicable and verifiable.
- It suits to the economic requirements of country like India. Basically science must be learnt by doing experiments but if that is not possible at least through demonstration children gets a chance to see the experiments. In these conditions the only method that helps children to learn science and to retain it for a longer time is demonstration method.
- Because of economic conditions and shortage of infrastructure facilities this method is suitable.

Steps of Lecture-cum-Demonstration Method

(1) It is a combination of both lecture and demonstration. The lecture is here interspersed by no. of experiments.

Step 1. Planning: A topic is first selected and studied its content is analyzed. Content Analysis is followed by formation of General and Specific objectives. Looking at the objectives method is selected. Say the topic is 'photosynthesis' learning experiences demand a demonstration of conditions required for photosynthesis.

So list of equipments

Materials

Chemicals
Procedure, place, time, duration is decided.
Next Step is

Step 2. Rehearse the planned demonstration. The rehearsal avoids any mistake and the element of practice boosts the confidence level of the teacher. It also helps to prevent failure of the demonstration.

Step 3. Actual Implementation of the Demonstration There are certain prerequisites that should be kept in mind before implementing a demonstration.

(i) Ensure that demonstration is visible to entire class. The demonstration table to entire class. The demonstration table should be higher than the desk of pupils.
(ii) Propcr lighting should be there.
(iii) Take pupils help in arranging the apparatus.
(iv) While explaining the demonstration use lucid language i.e. avoid any kind of ambiguity.
(v) Arrangement of apparatus should be from left to right, the used and unused material should be kept separately.
(vi) Size of the apparatus should be large, so that it is visible to entire class.
(vii) Demonstration should be based on season i.e., according to the availability of material.
(viii) There should be a blackboard summary with it.
(ix) Perform the experiment in batches
(x) Pace your performance, it should neither be too slow or fast
(xi) It is advisable to have a teaching aid to display the set up. So the other group can be involved in drawing and writing experiment.
(xii) Teacher should make it clear "what is to be observed and recorded?".
(xiii) Teacher must know how to repair simple instruments or how to adjust a simple instrument.
(xiv) Discuss how the principle learnt is useful in day to day life.

Next step is Evaluation: After demonstration. A discussion needs to be carried out. In this session the questions will be based on what is given?

How it was done? What happened? Why it happened? Where and How does it happen in our daily life?

In the discussion all students must be involved. What all things can be demonstrated?

(1) Demonstration of a microscope (a) Simple (b) Compound.
(2) Demonstration of various system of a frog.
(3) Demonstration of any dissection.
(4) Demonstration of parts of flower, etc.

Demonstration can be used at various stages

(1) To introduce osmosis.
(2) To explain photosynthesis transpiration, germination process.
(3) To have quick revision say parts of a plant, parts of a flower, a Bee colony etc.

Merits of Demonstration Method

(1) It is economical in the Indian context as no laboratory is required.
(2) As against laboratory which requires larger infrastructure demonstration requires much lesser finance and infrastructure.
(3) It makes the teaching learning process more concrete.
(4) The visual memory of students is helpful in retention, as more than one sense is used.
(5) It takes lesser time.
(6) It fulfills the aim of learning by doing.
(7) It has advantages of two methods, i.e., lecture and demonstration.

Demerit

(1) It gives no scope for hands on experience.
(2) It is dominated by teacher all the time.
(3) It does not cater to individual differences present among the students.

(4) Students do not develop laboratory skills through this method.
(5) All the students may not be able to observe the experiment.
(6) Even at the last discussion only a few students may participate. Some students may be left behind.

When a demonstration should be done?

(a) If the apparatus is fragile.
(b) If a new skill is introduced.
(c) If time is too short.
(d) If potential hazard is involved.
(e) To make the content interesting and live.

ASSIGNMENT METHOD

Apart from gaining minimum required knowledge from the presentations of teacher, the students are expected to identify various sources and acquire further knowledge. Also, they should develop certain necessary cognitive and attributes, skills, attitudes, etc. required for understanding responsibilities in the society. To achieve these objectives effectively it would be necessary to utilize certain instructional techniques through which they can get the opportunity to involve in certain independent activities. The large learners group demands the provision of variety of learning experiences according to their varied interests, abilities, aptitudes etc.

(1) Characteristics of Good Assignment: -

(a) It should be challenging and thought provoking. It should motivate and stimulate pupils. It should satisfy the curiosity and interest.
(b) Assignment should be from a lesson or unit, which they have learnt.
(c) Assignment should be in activity based.
(d) While giving assignment the teacher should keep in mind the individual differences of pupils their ability, interest, rate of learning etc.

(e) Language of the assignment should be simple, easy to understand.
(f) The sketches, graphs, charts, models should be given place in good assignment.
(g) Current events should have a place in assignment.

In the light of the nature of the learning experiences discussed above, it would be desirable to identify suitable instructional technique, which provide opportunity to the learners to work on their own. Assignment is a technique which can fulfill the above characteristics. According to DeSales (1976) the technique of assignment is useful because it (i) facilitates transition from one lesson to another, (ii) affects students' attitude towards learning, (iii) gives opportunity to pupils to plan and perform their work independently, (iv) is a valuable means of study without the restriction of a classroom and supplements the teaching work done in class, (v) Improves pupil's ability outside the schools, (vi) involves much repetition that is essential for fixing up the lesson that has been taught in class, (vii) develop the qualities of self-reliance, self-direction and initiation, and (viii) establishes a habit of reading regularly.

Types of Assignment

As discussed earlier assignments consist of student centred activities where the teacher's role is limited to providing certain guidelines. Even though assignments may encompass activities like practical work, library work, fieldwork, project work etc. it has an identity of its own. However, according to the type of activity taken up there can be various types of assignments. An attempt is made to classify them as follows:

(i) *Activity Centred Assignments:* In certain assignments the students perform some activities, observe carefully certain aspects of the activities, make inferences and thus come to the conclusions. These are then reported in a suitable way. In such assignments the suitable students may use the laboratory to conduct the activity or may do it in the field. Accordingly, the activity may be seen as a laboratory oriented activity or a field-oriented activity.

(ii) *Library Centred Assignments:* As indicated by the name itself these assignments would consist of students referring certain books in the library, integrating ideas and presenting as a write up along with ones own view points.

(iii) *Thought Provoking Assignments:* If certain problems or issues are provided, they can be discussed in a logical way to arrive at solutions or view-points. These solutions or viewpoints are reported along with necessary justifications.

Other Types of Assignment

1. Assignment based on observation and guided visits.
2. Assignment can be collaborated with radio talks, types, T.V. Internet, Etc.
3. Assignment on maps, pictures, charts, graphs, models, exhibits, etc.
4. Assignment based on excursions.

Remedial Assignment: - After conducting the unit test a teacher may find many students lack in some areas. For such areas a specialized drill assignment can be given to fill in the gaps in understanding if any.

Revisional Assignment: - Before examination an assignment is given to the students. This assignment acts as a preparation for the forth-coming examination.

Organization of Assignment

The organization of the assignments can be done keeping in view the following:

(i) *Selection of the Assignment:*- The selection of the type and theme of the assignment depends upon the nature of students, their entire behaviour, i.e., previous knowledge, interest, curiosity, intellectual level etc. This needs to be done on the part of the teacher at the planning stage and accordingly the suitable assignment should be decided. Such planning enables the placement of various other instructional inputs in relation to assignment. In order to motivate and awaken interests of the students the teacher selects interesting and stimulating topic for giving assignments. It would be meaningful to provide a variety of challenges (assignments) to meet the needs of learners whose temperaments differ and who have varying backgrounds. This means assignments should be individual (oriented) in character. Teacher may give a problem type of assignment in which the originality and creativity of the students is taken care of. Grouping of students could be done in order to take care of individual differences.

(ii) Preparation of the Assignment: The assignment should consist of the aim, details regarding ways to carry out, necessary guidelines for reporting etc. The language should be unambiguous and simple.

(iii) Setting Time Limits for the Assignments: Before giving the assignments, the teacher sets a time limit taking into consideration the nature of assignment and type of students like slow learners and fast learners, their maturity level, age level, etc.

(iv) Evaluating the given Assignment: Evaluation of assignment gives scope for the teacher to see the rate at which the students are doing the work assigned. Helps him to get a personal contact with the students, provides the students opportunities to solve the individual difficulties and to seek any other assistance from the teacher. In other words, evaluation of assignments does not begin only after the submission of the assignments but when it is in progress.

Merits

(1) It reduces the burden of teaching. Assignment makes learning meaningful, effective, and pinpointed to cover the course in time. It provides varied learning experiences.

(2) Assignment makes people work with zeal and enthusiasm.

(3) It develops some basic skills in pupils such as map reading, drawing, sketches, figures etc.

(4) To help pupils in taking relevant material from reference books.
(5) To help pupils to study and think independently.
(6) To help pupils in taking down important points from radio talks, Internet, T.V., expert talk, interview, discussion, etc.
(7) To help pupils in the power of observation.
(8) It develops self-study habit.

Demerits

(1) Without guidance assignment proves to be ineffective. It becomes burdensome to the students.
(2) Pupils feel tempted to copy down from their friends.
(3) There are possibilities of assignments becoming stereotyped.

Role of Teacher

In this method the teacher assigns the assignment according to the age and abilities of the students. The teacher must also look into the interest areas of various students, depending on their interest give them assignment.

LABORATORY METHOD

Theory evolves from practice, and practice consolidates theory. So to learn Biology or any other subject which is based on practice, practical are important. Whatever is taught in theory it is practiced in practicals. The theoretical input becomes more meaningful in practicals. First the theory is taught in classroom. In the laboratory brief description of the topic is given. Also the aim of experiment is given.

The teacher demonstrates the practical to the students. The students observe the teacher and learn the various skills involved in the practical, later the students individually perform the practicals themselves. It is based on the principle of learning by doing.

Importance of Laboratory Method

Steps involved in Laboratory Method: Preparation: - Before commencing the practical the teacher finishes teaching the relevant theoretical portion. This is followed by laboratory preparation. With the help of laboratory assistant the teacher organizes the practical before hand. If last two periods are practical in the previous class the teacher makes the arrangements in the laboratory. The suitable material is brought and arranged before the students enter the laboratory.

The teacher must do a rehearsal of the practical before hand.

Second Step: Demonstration for the students. The teacher demonstrates the practical to the students. On the blackboard there is brief summary of what is to be done and how. After viewing the demonstration the students go to respective places in the laboratory and carryout the given experiment.

The teacher must focus on what is to be seen. Teacher should also focus on various skills like use of dropper, stain, converslip, brush, forceps etc.

While performing the practical if any difficulty is faced by students they can consult their teachers.

Apart from this the teacher should give safety rules like handling instruments, chemicals, blades, etc. Also instruction needs to be given about first aid, if in case there is some accident what the students should do without creating panic. Teacher should also check journals and observation book.

Third Step: Recording: The students after completing the experiment have to note down their findings in the notebook. The students are also supposed to draw sketches in their notebook and get it signed by their teachers.

Fourth Step: Evaluation or discussion. The teacher at the end must carryout the discussion to find out whether all the students have clearly understood the concept and the skills for which the practical was organized. After the discussion students can get their journal and observation signed by the teacher.

Merits:

(1) It is based on the maxim of learning by doing.
(2) Understanding is concrete and retention is longer.
(3) The emphasis is on skill development.
(4) It helps in higher studies like medicine, agriculture etc.
(5) It clarifies the theoretical content.
(6) It develops psychomotor skills.
(7) It also develops social skills.
(8) It gives hands on training to students.
(9) One is able to understand the hard work and toil put forward by scientists.
(10) It develops scientific attitude, scientific method and scientific temper.

Demerit

(1) It is time consuming.
(2) It requires lots of resources.
(3) It disturbs environment.

Role of Teacher:

(1) Teacher must provide proper instructions.
(2) Teacher must provide proper facilities before going in the laboratory do rehearsal.
(3) Should give demonstration. If the demonstration fails one should be ready with another set of experiment.
(4) Should plan experiment according to the season.
(5) Some students who are intelligent finish the experiment very fast. So ask them to assist other students or to ask them to draw and write in the journal.
(6) Should make sure that each and every child is doing the practicals. It shouldn't happen that child is taking others work and if he does he can't gain the skills that have to be acquired.

(7) Should check their journals, observation notebooks, practicals, punctuality, and handling of apparatus.
(8) Should be a very good supervisor, a vigilant observer.
(9) Should motivate, encourage and bring enthusiasm in students.

HEURISTIC METHOD

This method was given by Prof. H.C. Armstrong (1968) who was a professor of chemistry at Imperial College London. He felt science must develop independent thinking. It must make its learners independent thinkers and discoverers. The word heuristic means to discover Sharma (1975) writes:

In the words of Prof. Armstrong, heuristic method is a method of teaching which involves our placing students as far as possible in the attitude of a discoverer.

Any method which excites children to work and think for them can be called heuristic method.

Any method which is opposed to dogmatic method of teaching in which pupils work and think for themselves; in which the habits of self-activity and self-dependence are fostered, is called the 'heuristic method of teaching.'

(a) Procedure

A sheet of instruction concerning a scientific problem is given to students and they are expected to undertake certain independent activities. For example—

(i) Taking observations independently;
(ii) Conducting experiments and taking observations independently;
(iii) Conducting experiments, taking observations and interpreting the results independently.

Main consideration of the above procedure is imparting training in the elements of scientific method of thinking. Westway rightly writes: 'Essentially, the heuristic method is intended to provide a training in method, knowledge is a secondary consideration altogether.'

During an independent work on a given problem, students are free to consult library, teachers, classfellows and any resource personnel in the community. Some authorities are of the view that a teacher should tell nothing to students and students should be helped follow instructions and work themselves independently. But, this is possibly an over expectation from students. A teacher should help whenever students feel the need for help a teacher should try to elicit an answer of a problem for students through well defined and relevant questions on a problem. Above all, problematic situation should be of such a nature that questions might come in the mind of students, while conducting experiments or undergoing a given assignment. In this way students will learn various elements of scientific method of thinking.

(b) Role of a Teacher

Prof. Armstrong emphasized that a teacher should give minimum and only most essential help to students; however, the modern views highlighted by different personalities are as follows:

(i) A teacher should help students to identify problems. If a problem is given to a students by a teacher, that should be according to the potential and availability of required resources.

(ii) Maintenance of interest of students in problems through constant inspiration and questioning technique is essential.

(iii) Personal ideas should never be imposed on students. Let them express their views and execute the same through trial and error method. Student will ultimately learn to solve a problem.

(iv) A teacher can organize field trips, excursions, visits to a museum, zoo, etc. which may contribute to a successful solution of a problem.

(v) A teacher can help in setting up experiments as a participant and guide.

(vi) A teacher should be a man of knowledge to give references to students.

(c) Merits

The most important advantage of heuristic method is the imparting of training to students in the various elements of a scientific method of thinking and to enable them to become independent thinkers. Westway has also mentioned that heuristic method is intended to provide training in scientific method and knowledge is a secondary consideration.

Some of the advantages listed below are nothing but the integral parts of the main goal, mentioned above. This method helps students to—

(i) think independently and solve problems;

(ii) develop the habit in following heuristic approach for solving day-to-day life problems;

(iii) ask questions of their interest and to secure answers;

(iv) develop the habits of self-activity and self-dependence.

(d) Demerits

Some important limitations of this method are as under:

(i) It is time consuming and very expensive as one will be in need of physical facilities and supplied for the solution of problems through experimentation and other activities like visits to concerned places.

(ii) Teachers are not fully trained in the approach and that is why they may not do justice in following this method.

(iii) Available instructional materials are not written on these lines for the guidance of teachers and students.

(iv) Above all, placing students in position of independent workers is something which seems to be extraordinary demand from students.

PROJECT METHOD

Project means a bit of real life which isn't theoretical or bookish. According to Kilpatrick, "A project is a unit of whole hearted purposeful activity carried on preferably in its natural setting". Project is a problematic situation which comes to completion with the required solution from school. Stresses the role of project to develop social skills. According to Stevenson "A project is a problematic act carried to its completion in its natural setting".

According to Ballard, "A project is a bit of real life that has been incorporated into the school.

Learning takes place in the natural setting. Students interact with nature.

Importance of Project Method:

It is based on the psychological principle of learning by doing. The learning gets consolidated faster. The concept can be learnt at depth involving various disciplines students learn creativity. They learn to solve problems. It emphasizes experiential learning.

Steps involved in project method.

1. **Providing a problematic situation**

   The problem should not be imposed on students. Teacher should provide interesting situations.

   (a) The teacher may organize field visits the students can be involved in collection of flora and fauna.

   (b) Different types of projects can be mentioned and students can opt for the project of their choice.

   (c) Teacher can demonstrate experiments to show importance of sunlight, chlorophyll etc.

   In the discussion students can be motivated to take up various experiments.

   (e) Silent demonstration can be placed in the laboratory or in the classroom for example an aquarium can be placed in the class or a potted plant. The new element in the class can raise questions in the mind of students.

(f) Certain wild life documentary, films can be shown to arouse interest.

(g) Discussion of content can be done which can arouse interest in students.

(h) Teacher may ask students to view a few Internet websites to generate interest in them.

Thus, in the given ways one can generate a problematic situation in front of students.

2. Selection of a Project

Student is able to sense the problems and depending upon interest, time and available resources plus the aptitude required for carrying it out.

The students after discussing common interest in a group – select a project. It is a group activity and a co-operative venture.

3. Planning: Planning in project is a group activity where the task at hand is thoroughly discussed. Students should be asked to read in the area of project. Students should consult people in the community and experts in the area. The project should be specified and further divided in the group so that people are given task according to their abilities and choices.

4. Execution: Meaningful implementation of planning is execution. The students' carryout the task after consulting with their teacher. The teacher guides the students whenever they have some difficulty. A teacher must see that every member is working independently and few members do not dominate the group.

5. Evaluation: Evaluation of the project should be two sided that the teacher evaluates the project plus the participants also evaluate their project in the light of given objectives. Evaluation of individuals' task is difficult, as it is a group effort.

6. Recording/Report:

Project Report is the end product and the compilation of the team effort. It must have following things.

1. Introduction.
2. Problem.
3. Hypothesis.
4. Methods and Material.
5. Experiment.
6. Results and discussion.
7. Summary.
8. References.

If it is visit to some site than pictures, specimen submission, herbarium preparation etc is to be submitted with the report.

A good project must keep in mind the age ability, interest, aptitude, and availability of time, resources, maturity, and individual differences that naturally exist among students.

Merits:

(1) It is based on the principle of learning by doing and learning by living.
(2) Understanding of the content is better.
(3) Students develop a lot of social skills.
(4) They learn to solve problems.
(5) They learn co-operative thinking and decision-making.
(6) Students learn self study habits.
(7) Students can develop scientific attitude and scientific temper.

Demerits:

(1) It is very time consuming.
(2) Expectations from teacher is very high.
(3) Good library is required to use this method.
(4) A good laboratory is also required to teach through this method.

Role of teacher:

The teacher in the project method plays many roles facilitator, motivator, guide, manager, helper, and supervisor.

The teacher first has to provide different situations to the students. Next the teacher must check the plan before execution to see that the leader of the group properly distributes the work after looking at the potentials of the members. The teacher also has to give deadline for the completion of the project. Finally, the teacher is supposed to evaluate and monitor the project report submitted by the students.

DISCUSSION METHOD

In a country like India, Lecture method may be largely indispensable due to the lack of resources or for whatever reasons discussed earlier. As we have adopted democracy as way of life, we cannot think of just one-way communication from teacher to student. Many time students want to tell something but his thoughts are thwarted in his mind. Active participation of students is possible by discussion method. This method is defined as a strategy for achieving instructional objectives that involves a group of persons usually in the roles of moderator and participants, who communicate with each other using speaking, nonverbal and listening process." Gall and Gillett, 1980. The broad objectives of this method are to allow students to articulate themselves cogently and in an organized fashion on any topic. At the same time it should develop in him the qualities of patience and tolerance, and a willingness to modify and rethink his own view in the light of arguments presented by others. It is therefore training in a group activity and co-operative thinking.

Importance of Discussion Method

The Discussion Method goes with the democratic philosophy that we have adopted. Where we first sit and discuss various matters at length and then reach a suitable decision.

Discussion has also become important now in selection and recruitment procedures where we have a scope for group discussion. Moreover, we know that a team can work together in a co-ordinated manner, when they have common understanding of issues. Common understanding makes it possible to clarify many issues and implement plan in more systematic manner. The students of higher secondary will be tomorrow's citizens so they must be made aware about the method and also they should be trained through this method of discussion.

Procedure involved: Discussion method can be carried out in two different ways.

(1) Entire group discusses on some issues after the teacher has taught.

(2) Discussion on the unknown topic area.

(1) Discussion after teaching the content

The most common type of discussion is the revisional discussion carried out by subject teacher it entails previous knowledge of the students about the content. After finishing the content. The teacher poses certain questions to the students and the students answer or sometimes teacher makes two groups' one-group poses questions to the other group. And turn-by-turn they ask questions and cover entire content.

(2) Discussion on the unknown topic

Here the teacher assigns new topics that have not been taught previously to a group of students. This group of students is then asked to go to library and prepare the content. The students are free to read and discuss with their teachers, friends, members of the community, doctors, they can also use Internet or any resource that is available. The task that the students are supposed to do is not very difficult but it should be according to their level and ability. Any student can gather information from any of the above mentioned sources in the given time framework. After judging the relevance of collected material one must collate and organize the given material properly. So that duplication of ideas and efforts can be avoided.

Group Leader: The Group leader must further specify and detail out work to the members in order to avoid work duplication. The leader must also see the potentials of the people in his group before further detailing the task. A student may be good in drawing, some may be good in talking accordingly there potentials can be tapped.

Members: Members must take direction from leader. After collecting the information they must give it to the leader for further compilation. The members must discuss and reach the decision in case of any confusion. If they cannot resolve, they can consult teacher or principal. The members also assist the leader in presentation.

Presentation Stage: After the preparation of draft by the group members. Presentation is made. The presentation is done by the leader. The presentation is followed by discussion where the audience poses questions to the speaker and the speaker responds to the queries. The queries are answered individually by the team members.

Evaluation: Evaluation in a discussion method is difficult as it is a group process. You as a teacher would not know who performed how. Because whatever you see is basically a group effort. In the revisional type of discussion evaluation of individual is not the Question. Because there what we want to judge is simply the understanding of the students about the content taught. But in the second type evaluation is possible on following criteria.

Criteria	*Weightage*
1. Content	40%
2. Style of presentation Voice, clarity of thought, Punctuation, references	15%
3. Teaching aids if any	5%
4. Responding to queries	20%
5. Report	20%

The criteria sheet could be given to both the students and the teachers and the average could be considered for evaluation. The teacher can also conduct viva of students to know what they have done and understood. The report is to be checked by the teacher.

Merits

(1) It develops skill of oral communication of ideas.
(2) It imparts information and changes attitudes.
(3) It clarifies student's difficulties.
(4) It helps students to think and train them in intellectual skills.
(5) It allows the students to share in the responsibility of presenting explaining and understanding ideas to allow them some measure of responsibility for their own learning.
(6) It allows students to let off steam about frustrations and problems.
(7) It gives students opportunity to consolidate their knowledge of ideas of concepts by trying them out and using the relevant terminology in discussion with their peers and tutor.
(8) It gives experience of working in a group, to tolerate ambiguity, patience, working in a co-ordinate manner.
(9) Training in co-operative thinking.
(10) Training in collective decision making process.
(11) Critical, analytical and reflective thinking are developed.

Demerits of Discussion Method

(1) If unmanaged it can get derailed.
(2) Individual task evaluation becomes difficult.
(3) If not controlled it can become chaotic and no understanding will be possible.
(4) One finds it highly time consuming.
(5) Sometimes it is not a healthy discussion but it simply becomes leg pulling exercise.

Role of a Teacher

The efficiency of the discussion is in the hands of a teacher. In discussion method teacher has to play multiple roles.

(1) Preparer, (2) Organizer, (3) Instructor, (4) Resource Controller, (5) Listener, (6) Observer, (7) Orienteer, (8) Motivator, (9) Supporter, (10) Manager, (11) Facilitator, (12) Summarizer.

Teacher must maintain democratic climate. The discussion should not be dominated by one group; all participants must get equal chance. Teacher should see that discussion does not go beyond the topic and loose relevance. Discipline should be maintained. Summary of discussion needs to be prepared. The teachers can supplement points given by the groups.

Topic for Discussion

(1) Pollution
(2) Population
(3) Diseases & Prevention

6
Approach

Introduction

The main aim of teaching is to bring about socially desirable behavioral change in the students and this can only be achieved if the teaching is effective and based on the principles of teaching. How the pupils will learn effectively, depends on the approach the teacher adopts. Teacher should have command on knowledge and skills of a variety of teaching methods and approaches. There is active interaction of science with problems in an interdisciplinary way which has provided newer insights. So there is need for a philosophy to conceptualize the newer approaches and organizing systematic experience to integrate knowledge into action. For this teaching of biology has undergone renewal through continuous interaction and acquisition of new and newer approach to add to problems in an innovative way. There are many new approaches used for teaching of biology and understanding of problems in a scientific perspective.

- ❖ Approach is a broad philosophy which is essential to study or follow a method.

There are various types of approaches: -

1. Inductive
2. Deductive
3. Inducto deductive
4. Inquiry
5. Science Technology & Society
6. Ecological
7. Integrated
8. Problem solving
9. Systems
10. Teleological

Every approach has got its own merits.

The choice of the approach depends upon the teacher, pupil and the content.

The effectiveness of teaching depends mainly upon the approach the teacher adopts. Teaching is an art and there are born teachers but a majority of the teachers have no inherent flair for teaching. For such teachers the knowledge of different types of methods and approaches of teaching is essential in order to improve expand their teaching by practice. There is a scope for combining one or more approaches compatible for realizing the objectives in the given situation. Teacher has the facility to understand more approaches to decide the right approach for the given content and situation. Self-learning and reflection are the 2 common elements in all the approaches to teaching described for implementing biology curricula.

Inductive approach

In this type of approach first number of illustrations are given to explain any concept that we come to generalization. When an array of facts or a series of informational material leads to generalization, the process is inductive. Inductive is a process of building from small sets of information's and illustration towards a major idea, principle or generalization. Through it, one is lead from concrete to abstract, particularly to general and from complex to general rule. One tries to prove universal law by showing that if it is true under one particular case, it is also in other similar cases. It examines each of sample or case under consideration and verifies properties for generalization though thinking for consistent result.

inductive
illustrations ————→ **generalization.**
approach

This type of approach is only possible when student has some previous knowledge about the concept. The students must have some exposure.

"Its an approach where we start from illustration and reach to generalization"

Illustration → Generalization.

Steps of Inductive approach.

↓

Observations

↓

Illustration

↓

Generalization

Pre-requisites

(1) The students should have some knowledge about the words, actions and reactions.

(2) They should have enough experience.

(3) They should also have a good amount of exposure.

Examples.

(1) Newton's third law.

Every action has an equal and opposite reaction to each other.

Teacher brings with her ball, rubber band now she asks the children to carefully observe her.

1. She throws the ball in the direction of wall.

The ball comes back to the teacher she asks the students: - 'I did an action what did you all observe;

One student says – The ball comes back after the action.

Teacher – Okay, now, she stretches the rubber band and leaves it. The students immediately spring up and say 'It has come back with some speed'

Teacher now says I have 60 kg weight and I am standing in this position, why isn't the floor giving away?

Student: - The floor is strong and so it has pushed you back.

Teacher: - Very good now if one of you push the other would that person push you back?

Students: - laugh, yes.

Teacher: - Why?

Students: - Because, he will be angry. So he will react.

Teacher: - Exactly so every action has an equal and opposite reaction. You all observed that the ball came back to me with the same speed as I had thrown it towards the wall. Similarly the elastic rubber was stretched to much an extent that it came back with a force. I push the floor so the floor pushes me back which is why I am able to stand in the same position. The floor has strength. Likewise when somebody is pushed or hurt, he too would gives it back with the same intensity. This is the Law of nature. So, today we have learnt Newton's Third law of Motion. 'That is every action has equal and opposite reaction.'

(2) Example.

Topic: Living organisms show adaptations.

Step: Giving known examples to students.

- Animals in desert generally are nocturnal. They have dry and thick skin. They store water. These are some adaptation of desert animals.
- Animals in water generally swim their body has large amount of water. They excrete ammonia. Plants in water have floating organs. They have aerenchyma tissue. Thus aquatic plants show some adaptation.
- Parasites respire anaerobically.
- Generally they have suckers. They have cuticle around their body. These are adaptation of parasites.
- Animals in polar region have furry skin. They have fatty layer beneath the skin. These are adaptations of animals in polar region.

Step II

These are different organisms. Showing different environmental different types of adverse condition are there to overcome these condition they have some physiological, physical, changes in their body we call them adaptations.

Step III Generalization.

Thus different organization for their environment show some adaptations.

Living organization show adaptations.

Example (4) Pollution.

- Smoke from chimneys.
- Are chimney gases desirable?
- What happens when large garbage is dumped?
- No. of vehicles plying on road gases and amount of noise etc.

Example (5) Population growth and control.

- Problems faced by India.

Pollution, Poverty unemployment.

↓

Population growth → effect → social effect / economy / Natural resource

Explain all the effects at the end talk of control.

Merits

(1) It breaks monotony of the class.

(2) As children have some activity they learn from surrounding.

(3) Curiosity increases.

(4) Inculcates scientific attitude.

(5) It helps understanding, scientific method, development of scientific attitude. It is logical in approach which develops critical thinking and habit of keen observation. It provides ample scope for students activities, based on actual observation, thinking and experimentation, help keeping alive the students, curbs tendency of rote learning. It develops self-confidence, develops habit of intelligent hard work.

Disadvantages:

- Time consuming.
- All contents cannot be taught by this method.

2.Deductive Approach

Deductive approach has a logical basis to infer some relationship as a hypothesis or theory. It depends on scientific evidences obtained through experimental method. The hypothesis arrived from deductive approach can be tested in the laboratory through experimental method or observed in nature over long period of time for obtaining consistent results.

If the students are not exposed to the surroundings or to the outer world then we cannot follow inductive approach because they didn't know at all. Thus we proceed from generalization to illustrations.

We give them general law, Theory or Principle and based on that we give number of examples.

3. Inquiry Approach

This approach is a pupil-centred approach. In this type of approach students ask questions to the teacher and then they make a conclusion. This approach is followed by a discrepant event.

Teacher does a demonstration or she/he draws diagram on the blackboard from which students get puzzled and formulate questions, which have 'yes', or 'no' answers. After collecting all 'yes' type of answers students reach to conclusion.

Later students can perform the experiment and verify result.

Procedure

Here teacher presents a puzzling event.

For example

glass filled with water water does not spill.

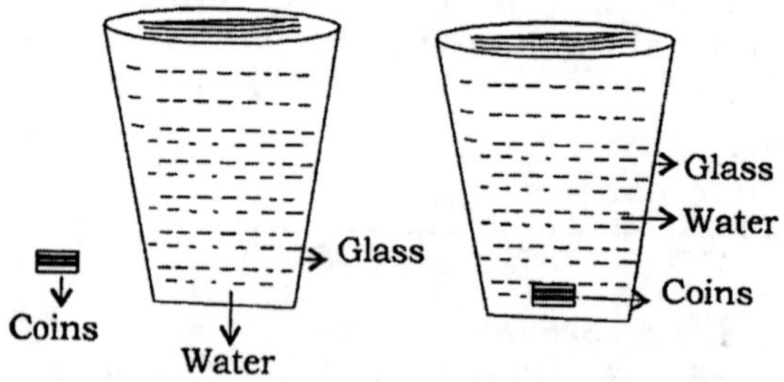

Picture 2 Water Doesnot overflow from the glass even when coins are immersed in it.

- Then students ask questions related to that event and teacher gives answer either in 'yes' or 'no'.
- Students make a **list** of answer of 'yes' and 'no'. Answers.
- Students come to the main target point with the help of answers.
- Now students perform experiment on their own and verify their results to come to a conclusion.

Example 1

Teacher: - Observe the experiment carefully and tell me which process I am demonstrating.

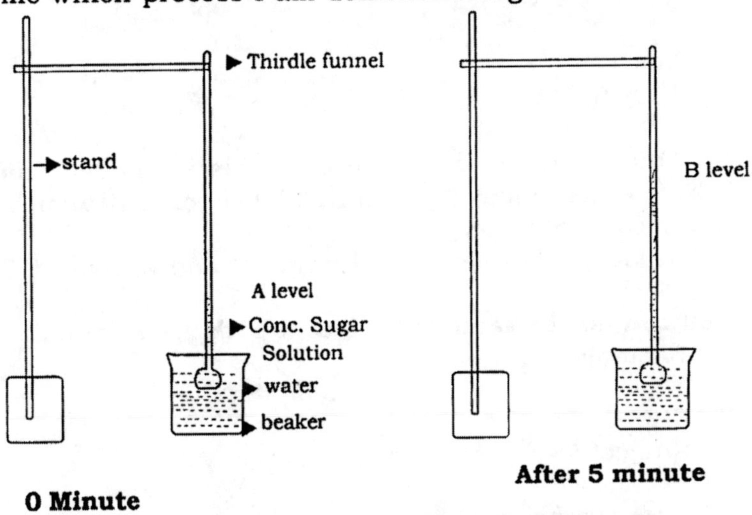

Picture 3. Thistle Funnel Experiment to show Osmosis.

Inquiry Starts

(1) Student. Is this universal phenomena? Teacher: - Yes.

(2) Student. Is this related to water? Teacher: - Yes

(3) Student. Is this related to evaporation? Teacher: - No.

(4) Student. Is this related to effect of temperature on water? Teacher: - No.

(5) Student. Is this related to effect of pressure on water? Teacher: - Yes.

(6) Student. Is it related to water movement? Teacher: - Yes.

(7) Student. Is this absorption? Teacher: - Yes.

(8) Student. Do we get same result if water is there in both thistle funnel and beaker? Teacher: -No.

(9) Student. Do we get same result if sugar solution was in beaker and water in thistle funnel? Teacher: - No.

(10) Student. Is this Osmosis? Teacher: -Yes.

(11) Student. Is this endosmosis? Teacher: - Yes.

Students' record.

Yes	No
1, 2, 6, 10, 5	3, 4, 7, 8, 9

Thus students conclude that this is endosmosis. Where water is moving from its higher concentration to lower concentration.

Students now perform experiment and verify.

You can do the same experiment with dry raisins.

Example

Topic: - Properties of Metal

Std.: - VIII

Subject: - Science.

Here teacher performs an experiment and shows to students.

Teacher: -The teacher will explain the three Test tubes, in brief and ask them to observe carefully.

Ask Questions which have Yes/No answers.

Students: - Madam in second Test Tube iron does not rust as there is No water;

Teacher: - Yes.

Students: - 2nd case it is because nail is totally immersed inside water.

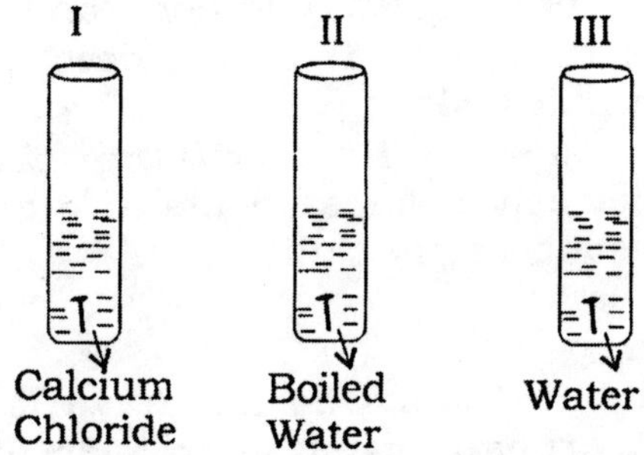

Picture 4 Test Tubes Containing Nails and Various Solutions.

Teacher: No.

Students: In the Ist case it is not rusted because of presence of calcium chloride.

Teacher: Yes

Students: IInd case water is boiled so no rusting.

Teacher: Yes.

Students: In boiling water there is no O_2

Teacher: Yes.

Students: In 1st case moisture is absorbed by calcium chloride.

In IIIrd O_2 and moisture are present from water so rusting occurs.

Teacher: - Yes.

Student:- Iron gets rusted in presence of O_2 and H_2O.

Why the coupling or water pipes are protected from rusting. Magnesium plates are used.

Why the base of ships does not rust?

Merits

- It emphasizes on learning by doing.
- The students tend to remember the content for a longer duration, thus it promotes retention.
- It is based on scientific method, where a student is expected to hypothesize and find a solution for the problem.
- There is involvement of scientific approach in solving the puzzle.

- Students develop scientific attitude, they do not accept the given conditions, and they try to think for themselves thus they develop reasoning and thinking skills.
- By personally verifying the experiment themselves the students also get a practice in the laboratory skills.

Demerits

- The textbooks do not have much scope for Discrepant event moreover for every topic discrepant event is not possible.
- As it involves student's participation it becomes Time Consuming.
- Not economical.

4. Science technology and society (STS) Approach

Allows individual to understand the interaction of :-

Science
Technology
Society

To create citizens who understand science and technology as Multidisciplinary and Multidimensional.

This would enable them to participate in critical thinking.

How science and technology are implemented and alter society and the environment.

- How science influences teaching of science and teacher and social institution?.
- Knowledge of concepts.
- Awareness of scientific Method.
- Ability to know science and technology related social and Environment Issues.

The objectives are.

1. Offer opportunity for student to compare and contrast science and technology.
2. Illustrate example of how science and technology knowledge is acquired.

- Include knowledge of science and technology in the context of day to day experiences of student.

Adaptations

STS is human and society focused

This approach is an attempt to study science technology and their impact on society. Science and technology have given many benefits to society at but the same time they have created many problems related to ecology and environment. All these topics related with science, technology and society could be taught through STS approach.

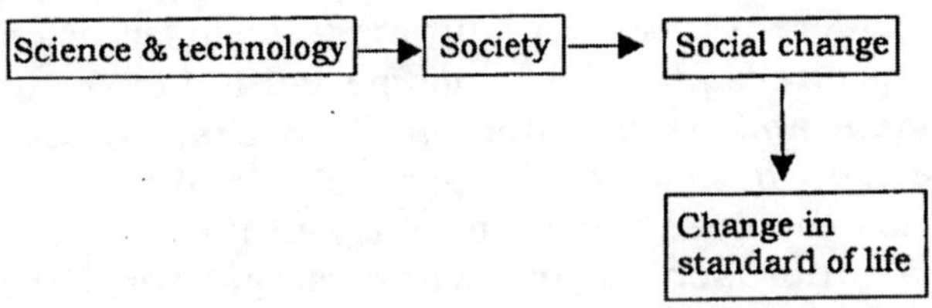

Example : - (1) More and More accuracy in measurement is a demand of society.

- Development of different instruments is a reply of science and technology.

(2) Transportation should be extremely fast and comfortable is a demand of society.

- Development of various means of transportation is a reply of science and technology.

⇒ **Application:** - When we teach any topic through this approach we see both positive and negative impacts of any scientific and technological development on society.

Example : advantages and disadvantages.

⇒ **Prerequisites:** - For STS approach knowledge of scientific concept is necessary. Awareness about general science is required. We should also know about social and environmental issues.

Merits

(1) Allows individual to understand the interaction of science, technology and society in order to create citizens who understand science and

technology in multidisciplinary and multidimensional ways.

(2) This would enable them to participate in critical thinking, how science and Technology when implemented brings change in society and environment?

5. Ecological Approach

The content of biology harbours many environmental issues like pollution, green house effect, water pollution, air pollution, noise pollution, garbage management etc. All these different types of pollution and conservation of natural resources plus the topics pertaining to the area of biosphere and its maintenance can best be taught with the help of ecological approach. In most of the approaches the question that we try to answer is how ecological approach is one where a teacher sites a problem related to environment. Students here try to find the why aspect of the environmental issue and also try to solve the problem at hand. Thus trying to solve the environmental problem faced by the humanity.

Ecological approach which focusses on the environmental issues and problem. It has been decided that environmental education has to be taught through interdisciplinary as well as multidisciplinary manner. This can best be done by the ecological approach. We always have some frame of reference in teaching, i.e., environment, its preservation, and its conservation. Any topic taught through this perspective falls under the ecological approach.

For example, carbon, water, oxygen, nitrogen cycle, renewable resources, solar energy, population problem, acid rain etc.

Ecological approach aims at instilling values to bring about change by organizing action plans exhibitions etc. with direct, indirect connection to environmental values.

It can be done in two ways.

Classroom Approach: By organizing field trips and asking questions to students why such a problem has come up? Who is responsible? Who is the beneficiary? Who will sensitize the students to take more responsible action for sustainable development?

For example Teacher can ask questions about global warming. Why the temperature variations are occuring on globe. What is the cause for the global warming? Based on the teachers questions students may discuss it further.The second approach is more suitable for higher standards. The group is given work and the students are expected to find the results by framing hypothesis and further researching the topic.

A. Is the classroom activity while approach B is basically a field activity.

Example of B field approach. The students are given the problem to study vegetation in different regions, i.e., in garden, near residence, on hill side, in desert, near traffic signal, near the industry, on the bank of river. In and around Baroda the students move and make the study on how the size, height and colour vary for the same plant in different location also try to study the reasons that are responsible for such factors.

6. Integrated Approach

It is used when a content has to be taught to students with the integration of many other topics. It is bridging the problem and theory many topics have to be used to teach the concept of a particular content. The topics in this content could be from different subjects. After teaching they should look like a unified whole.

For example teaching of Environmental Problem. This can be looked from Physics, Chemistry, Biology, Social Studies.

The biggest environment problem of pollution. There are different types of pollution, which is caused by the industries, i.e., (Chemistry).

The pollution caused is directly affecting human beings and animals (Biology).

The various parameters which are used to detect The Standards and the limits is contribution by the (Physics), example of the noise pollution limit which is having units called decibel.

The various diseases caused by air pollution and water pollution. Which is causing damages to our body system we need to study how pollution is caused what are the chemical components of the air pollution. The biggest killer carbon monoxide how and why it has the greater affinity to bind to the hemoglobin and why O_2 cannot so easily mix when the CO in our body is more. We need to study the chemical combination of these gases.

Similarly, when noise pollution is caused which part of the ear is getting disturbed and destroyed what is the range of sound, which is bearable to us. This deals with the wave studies that are in physics.

Similarly in the biotechnology there are various instruments used like centrifuge spectrometer, laminar flows etc. The bio students are supposed to study function of these instruments and appliances.

The combination of medium for the tissue culture approaches. If any compound is added more or less than the entire work is of waste. So teacher need to put these things in an appropriate and integrated manner that students get the knowledge of all the subjects so that it is the general awareness education and he/she needs to be expert in all the field. Today education is interdisciplinary.

3rd when we have to teach the agricultural practices and agriculture we need to study geographical condition like the soil type, climate temperature atmosphere, humidity etc.

Orchids are epiphytes needing humid conditions.

Use of micropipettes and burettes and their reading have to be taken to study BOD and COD and titrations.

Thus bio can be taught in integrated manner.

Structure of Eye: - This topic can be taught using biological and physics aspects (subject).

Biology: - Structure of eyes – Cornea, pupils, Iris, ciliary muscles, retina, aqueous humous, vitrous humour, Red cells and cone cells etc.

Physics: - The working/functioning of eye can be taught as. The lens is convex lens when the person is suffering from Myopia (Short Sightedness)

Hypermetropia (long Sightedness).

The focal length of the lens is increased and decreased respectively.

Myopia: - can be corrected by using concave lens so that the focal length gets decreased and the image will be formed on the retina. Similarly the Hypermetropia where the image is formed in front of retina can be corrected by using convex lens so that it forms on the retina.

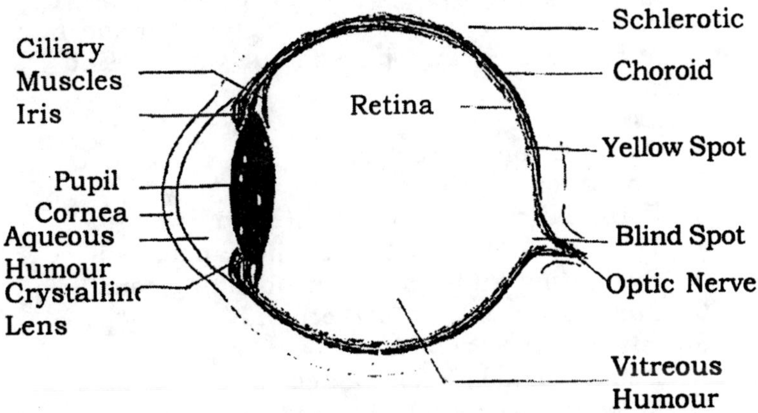

Picture 5. Structure of Eye

Osmosis

Biology: It is a biological phenomenon, which is useful in transport of material in living organism.

The process of movement of solvent molecules from the region of lower solute concentration towards the solution having higher solute concentration across a semi permeable membrane is called as osmosis.

Chemistry: - Cell membrane (semi permeable) solution (Hypertonic solution). In this solution the concentration of solute is less in the beaker than the cell itself so the solvent will move from the region of higher concentration of solute, i.e., the cell to the solution and it gets shrunk.

In Isotonic solution the concentration of both the solution are same so no movement of solvent will take place.

In Hypotonic solution the concentration of solute is more in the beaker than the cell so the solvent from the beaker moves into the cell and it gets swollen.

8. Problem Solving

In problem solving approach the activity involved leads to a mental solution. What is problem solving? Problem solving is an approach in which the felt difficulty to act is realized and then an attempt is made in a conscious, planned and purposeful way to find its solution.

Steps

1. Formulation of problem
2. Collection of relevant data
3. Formulation of tentative solution
4. Testing and verification of the conclusion
5. Evaluating findings and establishing conclusion
6. Summarization for further study

Selection of the Problem

- Definite educational values
- Related to the students need
- Real challenge
- Clearly stated
- Not difficult nor easy

Teacher's Role

- The classroom atmosphere should be free and friendly.
- The teacher needs to provide intelligent guidance to the students.

Advantages

- Useful throughout career.
- It gives fine chance to think, evaluate, compare, select the best logical way of thinking.
- Focus on knowledge of students.

- Develops qualities related to problem solving.
- Good harmonious relationship.

Disadvantages

- It may become monotonous
- Student misunderstand
- Intellectual training is less.

One of the main objective of education is to help students in solving problem during his life time. It is hoped that they can apply their minds and principles according to situation. For example at room temperature.

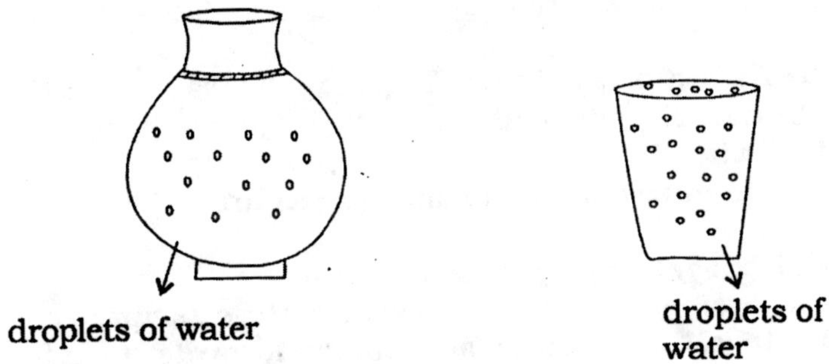

Picture 6. Water containers at room Temperature.

1. Identifying the problem

Why water droplets are formed?

2. Relevant data

Has it to do with hole in pot or metal?

3. Formulating hypothesis (Tentative solution)

"May be the vessel has holes"

"May be there is temperature difference"

"May be there is condensation"

4. Testing and verifying the hypothesis by framing various experiments

5. Evaluating finding

There is condensation due to temperature difference.

6. Further study

Experiment of boiling water can be performed.

Experiment with ether can be performed.

9. Systems Approach

Meaning of system: -

1. A system is a whole composed of some different component, which are interrelated.

2. A system can also be defined as "organized or established procedures, i.e., the ideas, principles, methods, procedures have been methodically arranged, e.g., solar system, e.g. The arrangement is systematic.

Example Human body has number of subsystems, which are working in, inter dependent and inter related way then only body functions. If there is problem in one part it is felt by entire body.

Defining a system: A system is "a regularly interactive or independent group of items forming a unified whole"

"an organized or established procedure".

What is a systems Approach?

The systems approach is a systematic attempt to co-ordinate all aspects of a problem towards specific objectives.

(1) Systems approach is a rational problem solving method of analyzing the educational process and making it more effective". It's being applied in education i.e. when ever there is any problem in education this approach is used.

(2) System is the process taken as a whole incorporating of all its aspects and parts viz, pupils, teacher curriculum, instructional material, strategies, physical environment and evaluation of instructional objectives.

(3) System approach is one of the techniques which aims at finding the most efficient and economically interconnected method for solving the problems of education scientifically.

(4) System is an assembly of objects/units with interactions and interdependence collectively contributing towards overall complex function.

Characteristics of a System

System comprises parts/components called as sub system, i.e., the parts that make the whole system. Each system may be sub system of a larger whole.

For example Society is a system, education is sub system. Body is system, respiratory, circulatory, digestive etc. are the sub systems.

2. Any change in one system is visible in the other subsystems. Because they are interlinked with each other.

3. Synergy/co-operation: It means working with each other by collecting each and everybody's strength. All the sub system if co-operates and work effectively then it will yield better results.

4. Competition: Competition may not be applicable in living system. Competition is usually where the resources are limited.

5. Field of Enablement: This simply means that systems are in the environment which has the potential to sustain other life forms also. If in this environment there is an organism, then it enables many other life form to sustain survive. In other words the environment has potential to sustain variety of life forms by providing their demands. In the same environment all life forms coexist.

6. Flow: There will be flow of material from the environment into the system. When the material is coming into the system there occurs some transformation process and output comes out of the system.

7. Feedback: It is the positive and negative feedback which affect the working of a system.

The systems approach means first focusing on learner and the performance required of him and then and only then, making decisions about course content learning experiences and the most effective media and instructional tactics.

In systems approach there are two processes which are normally used. Viz.,

(a) System design

(b) System analysis.

System design: It is the process used in constructing/making new system/model. For designing a system there are many steps. (Stevenson 1968)

1. Setting the objectives.
2. Delimit the scope of system.
3. Thinking of possible subsystem and their inter relationship and feasibility.
4. Modeling of sub-system.
5. Try out the modeled system.
7. Construction of the final system.

Steps Involved in System Analysis

1. To analyze the existing situation: It means to analyze the problem, i.e., what's the problem in existing system.

2. To step up a goal for a desired situation, i.e., to set objectives. One has to improve the system by setting goals.

3. To define the mechanism to evaluate the achievement of goals: How to evaluate, e.g., either through testing at that stage.

4. To create alternative solution: - For every problem there's solution. Any decision-making situation has problem then take a solution. Here many solutions are created and then choose the best possible solution.

5. To select most appropriate solution their cost benefit analysis: - Here, choose the best solutions by doing this one has to keep in mind the cost benefit, i.e., whether the cost spend is worth and will the benefit be the same as the cost.

6. Detailing the design of a system: - Whatever the design a system has detail and design of the subsystem.

7. Outlining the monitoring mechanism for the system: - Here monitoring is equal to evaluation, i.e., whether the system is working properly or not.

Uses of Systems Approach

1. It provides a conceptual framework on which one builds plans for implementing change in education, i.e.,

systems approach gives a skeleton outline on how to proceed further.

2. It helps to identify the suitability otherwise of the resource material to achieve the specific goals, i.e., helps to judge whether the resources are available, are they producing any hindrance for designing the innovation.for bringing any change that is to be brought.

3. Technological advances could be used to provide integration of machines, media and people for attaining the defined goals.

4. It permits an orderly introduction of components required for system success in terms of logical systematic manner in the system for enhancement of the main objective, which is for system learning.

5. Rigidity in plan/is avoided as continuous evaluation helps in the desired changed to be made, i.e., if rigidity is avoided therefore at every step continuous evaluation is present and so feedback is also continuous which helps in desirable changes of the system. Thus, a new and modified system is made.

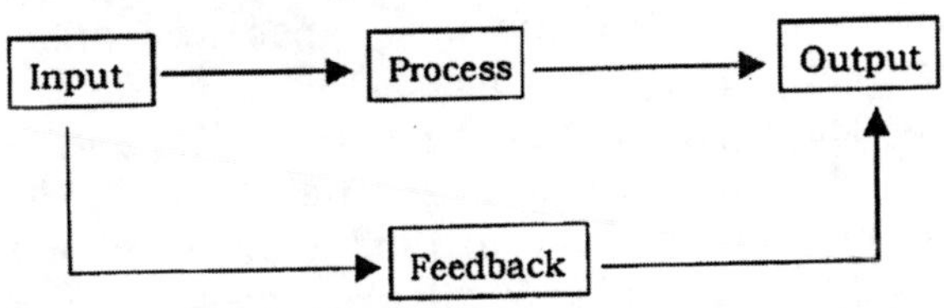

Error signal generator

10. Teleological Approach

There are two main features that differentiate biology from physical sciences.

1. Dominant place occupied by teleological explanation in biological inquiry.
2. Use of conceptual tools uniquely appropriate in the study of systems whose total behavior is not the resultant of the activities of independent components.

Teleological Analysis is understood to be an inquiry into such functions and into processes, which are directed toward attaining certain end products.

Teleological explanation for example " The function of chlorophyll in plants is to enable plants to perform photosynthesis" This is teleological explanation as it has structure and function. But plants perform photosynthesis only if they contain chlorophyll is a non-teleological explanation as it does not have structure function relationship.

Analytical methods of natural science are competent for study of non-living things. Despite the undeniable success of physico chemical explanations in the study of living things biologists consider them to be not entirely adequate for the subject. Mode of analysis required for understanding living phenomena is fundamentally different. Biology has long been arena in which crucial issues in the logic of explanation have been the subject of vigorous debate. Explanatory concepts in biology are distinctive of science and that biology is an inherently autonomous discipline. There is difference between the living and non living. Biology studies anatomy and physiology of living things. It classifies vital organisms into types and species and studies evolutionary changes.

Analyzes organism as structure to interrelated parts and seeks to discover what each part contributes to the maintenance of the organism as a whole. Biology requires special skills. Vital processes have a prima facie purposive character; for organisms are capable of self-regulation, self maintenance and self reproduction and other activities seem to be directed towards the attainment of goals lie in the future.

Morphological study is one part later inquires into functions of structures in sustaining activities of the organisms as a whole goal directed behavior of living things is often regarded as requiring a distinctive category of explanation in biology. Living things are organic wholes, not additive systems of independent parts and the behavior of these parts cannot be properly understood if they are regarded as isolated mechanisms. The parts of an organism must be viewed as internally related members of an integrated whole. They influence each other. Two main features are commonly alleged to differentiate biology from physical science. One is dominant place occupied by teleological explanation in biology inquiry.

Other is the use of conceptual tools. Teleological specifies the functions. The function of chlorophyll in plants is to enable plants to perform photosynthesis, Teleological statement.

However A necessary condition for the occurrence of photosynthesis in plants is the presence of chlorophyll a non-teleological statement. When a function is ascribed to a constituent of some organism, the content of the teleological statement is fully conveyed. Difference between teleological and non teleological explanation is thus comparable saying that B is an effect of A. A is a cause or condition of B. Selective attention rather than asserted content. The function of the leukocytes in human blood is to defend the body against foreign microorganisms. Teleological statement explanation implies non-teleological one. It is for teaching of biology. Biology is not any physical and chemical property but some extra property of livingness is involved in it. The basic property of living is to produce effective and efficient progeny from generation to generation. Biology is different from physics and chemistry. Teleological approach is the application inquiry type of function related to some assumption we are having. Every part has some function and if function changes the part is also changing. An approach which, is from reverse side is called teleological approach. For a system approach we see part and then function here we first see the function and then the parts, i.e., it is from tail to head:

1. Observe the living organism and phenomena
2. Analyze its function
3. Arrange all the activities performed in the function necessary for the system to live.
4. Reason out how the alternative selected by the organism is suitable since the organism goes on changing depending on the environment.

7
Models of Teaching

- Teaching is an abstract concept and not a concrete concept.
- It is systematic process which intends to induce learning.
- Joyce Bruce and Marsha Weils prepared well-defined models of Teaching.
- Model is a replica of the real object and has similar color and appearance.
- Teaching does not have systematic steps, so to define if one has to make teaching systematized and standardized. This will help to make a Model of Teaching.
- Model of Teaching is just instructional designs.
- They describe the process of specifying and producing a particular environmental situation, which causes the students to interact in such a way that specific change occurs in his behaviour.
- Models consist of guidelines for designing educational activities and environment.

Joyce Bruce defined model of Teaching, as "it is a plan that can be utilized to shape courses of studies to design instructional material and to guide instructions."

Model has 3 strategies viz. design of curriculum, instructional material and instruction. If one is able to organize these 3 strategies and knows what plan is to be followed, then that pattern or design is model of teaching.

Methods of Teaching: It is the process of techniques used for giving instruction in a special way, 2/3 lectures can be compared on the basis of presentation of content and the style.

- There can't be comparison between two lectures and
- There cannot be replication of methods of teaching.

Model of Teaching:

- Model is the outline replica/generalized plan of realia having characters of real things.
- When model of teaching is to be considered then one should be aware of the nature of teaching.
- Teaching is a systematic process, which has number of actions and activities.
- The objective and the product of teaching are learning and it can produce a conducive learning climate.
- To organize a structured and standardized process, where there are number of activities organized for enhancing learning, model is thus created.
- In Methods of Teaching also number of activities are organized, e.g., when a teacher delivers lecture, the style of delivering lecture, it is same every time?

  The style of lecturing may vary from time to time and from teacher to teacher.
- Model of teaching has definite steps, which can be followed by the teacher.
- Models of teaching are based on definite verified, predecided principles. It is a generalized plan of teaching.
- It includes directions of how instructions are to be performed and also tells how curriculum and instructions are developed.

Model of Teaching	*Method of Teaching*
It is not a way of presentation but a generalized plan	It is a way of presentation.
It is based on same verified and clearly spelt out principles/strategies.	It is not based on verified principle.

The strategies are centred on objectives.	
The outcome is important.	There is no such implication.
It is well structured.	It is not so much structured.
Its steps are replicable. There are definite steps to be followed.	There are no steps, which can be replicable.
It has definite and precise rules and regulations.	No definite rules.
It is rigid.	It is flexible.
It is pupil centred.	It is teacher and content centred.
Students are active and they take decisions teachers are less active.	No flexibility for decisions
Roles and responsibilities of students and teachers are clearly spelt out.	There are no specifications for students and teachers.
Includes direction of how instructions are performed and also tells how curriculum and instruction is developed.	Such a thing is not there.

Classification of Models of teaching in 4 families: Information Processing Model. (IPM)

Information is the knowledge of something /number of stimulus which are responsible for providing information. It can be from people, friends etc. IPM tells us how we process the information, how our mind works. The process of getting the information is a neutral process.

- It is different from individual to individual.
- Here information is provided by teacher and then it is processed in child's mind.
- It is also provided by paper, TV, media etc.
- In short it is about how an individual receives an information and how he/she learns from it.

Example Teacher is source of information and when there is examination some student write similarly what teacher said, some in their own words according to their understanding level etc.

This family refers to the ways people handle stimuli from the environment; organize data, sense problems, generated concepts and solutions to problems and employ verbal and non-verbal symbols.

- It emphasizes abilities of solving problem, general intellectual ability. The route chosen is through, intellectual functioning.

Personal Models:

- It has orientation towards the individual and development of selfhood.
- They emphasize the processes by which individuals construct and organize their unique reality.
- They give attention to emotional life.
- They view themselves as capable persons.

Social Interaction Models:

- The models of this family emphasize the relationships of the individual to society or to other persons.
- Models from this orientation give priority to the improvement of the individual's ability to relate to others to engage in democratic processes and to work productively in the society.
- Though the prime aim is social interaction it also aims at development of mind, self and learning of academic subject.

Behaviour Modification Model:

- The thrust is an emphasis on changing the visible behaviors of the learner rather than the underlying psychological structure and the unobservable behaviour.
- Behaviour models are applied in education, training, interpersonal behaviour and therapy.
- It is based on stimulus control and response.

- They include models for teaching facts, concepts and skills reduction of anxiety and getting relaxation.
- The behavioural models break down the learning tasks into a series of small, sequenced behaviours.
- The control is in the hands.

IPM. That we will learn are: -

1. ITM - Inquiry training Model J. Richard Suchman. Model is based on cause and effect.

2. CAM - Concept attainment model.
Jerome Bruner based on process of thinking

Concept for describing a Model:

Each Model has 4 sections.

1. Orientation to the Model.
2. The model of teaching.
3. Application.
4. Instructional and nurturant effects.

(1) Orientation will have
- Goals of the model
- Theoretical assumptions
- Principles and major concepts

(2) Second sections present's
- Syntax
- Social system
- Principle of reaction
- Support system

(3) Third Section: Provides application and information about the use of model in the classroom, sometimes illustrations.

(4) Finally to summarize there is a short section on instructional and nurturant learning's that can be expected from the model.

(1) Syntax: - Describes the model in Action for, e.g., if teachers were to use the model as the basis for their strategy what kinds of activities would they use? How would they begin? What would happen next? Each model has distinct flow of phases.

(2) The Social System: The social system describes students and teachers roles and relationships and the kind of norms that are encouraged. The leadership roles of a teacher vary greatly from model to model.

(3) Principles of Reaction: Tells the teacher how to regard the learner and how to respond to what the learner does. Principles of reaction provides the teacher with rules of thumb and which to tune in to the student and select model - appropriate responses to what the student does.

(4) Support System: We use this concept to describe not the model itself so much as the supporting conditions necessary for its existences. What are the additional requirements of the model beyond the usual human skills and capacities and technical facilities? Support is in the form of books, films, self-instructional systems and travel arrangement's is necessary or the model will be empty.

(5) Instructional and Nurturant Effect: The effect of environment can be direct - designed to come from content and skills on which activities are based or an Implicit Effect. The examination of latent functions can be as important as the examination of direct functions.

Direct/Instructional Effects-

Indirect/Nurturant Effects.

The instructional effects are those directly achieved by leading the teacher in certain directions.

The nurturant effects come from experiencing the environment created by the model.

For example High competition may directly spur achievement but the effect of living in competitive atmosphere may alienate people from each other.

Here **Achievement** is Instructional Effect **Alienation** is a Nurturant Effect.

Inquiry Training Model (ITM)

The emphasis of the ITM is upon in inquiry process though structuring and re-structuring of the questions and sequencing them appropriately. The questions are based on inductive or deductive reasoning.

- Richard Suchman - to describe unusual phenomena e.g. light bulb blows off.

Orientation of the Models

(a) Goals and Assumptions.

(i) People inquire naturally when they are puzzled.

(ii) They can become conscious of and learn to analyse their thinking strategies.

(iii) New strategies can be taught directly and added to the students existing ones.

(iv) Co-operative inquiry enriches thinking and helps students to learn about the tentative and emergent nature of knowledge and to appreciate alternative example.

(b) Overview of the **Teaching Strategy:**

E.g. bending of the blade.

The emphasis is on mastering the inquiry process and not the content.

THE MODEL OF TEACHING

Syntax of ITM:

Phase one Encounter with Problem	Explain inquiry Procedures present discrepant event	A puzzle, riddle or magic trick. Discrepancy is that it involves illogical phenomena that conflicts our notion.
Phase two Data Gathering verification	Verify the nature of objects and conditions verify the occurrence of the problem situation. Ask what?	Students gather information about the event they see or experience. Students should get out of 'throw away' the variable may be useful later. - It can be misleading Questions about objects, properties, condition and events. Objects refers to determining nature of objects. (e.g., Is the knife made of steel?)

		Condition refers to state of object or systems, e.g. (was the blade hotter)? Properties refers to verifying the behavior of objects, e.g. (Does copper always bend when it is heated)?
Phase three Data Gathering Experimentation.	Isolate relevant variables. Hypothesize (and test) causal relationships. If and than	
Phase four Formulating an Explanation.	Formulate rules or explanation.	Group can shape the explanation that fully responds to the problem.
Phase five Analysis of the Inquiry process.	Analyze inquiry strategy and develop more effective ones.	Questions that were most effective, productive - those were not proper - some information which they couldn't obtain. This phase is essential if we are to make the inquiry process a conscious one and systematically try to improve it.

Social System:

STUDENT

The classroom environment should be

- Co-operative
- Participative
- Structured teacher controlled initially.
- Open to all relevant ideas
- Students participate as equals.
- Gradually it can be student controlled where student can discuss and study resource material
- Open CR setting

TEACHER

- Presents the problem situation
- Referee's the inquiry procedures
- To respond to students inquiry
- Establish focus on inquiry
- To facilitate discussion

Principles of Reaction:

The teacher responds in Yes or No. If a student formulates a question which cannot be answered in Yes or No. Teacher must ask the students to rephrase the Question in such a way that it has Yes or No answer.

Teacher can, if necessary, give new information by focusing on particular problem.

Support System:

Discrepant Events and Resource material

Teacher should develop inquiry material themselves.

Application

It can be used in any subject area in which a discrepant event can be presented.

In planning for discrepant event two primary factors should be considered.

(a) Problem requiring an Explanation. (Why?)

(b) Match the difficulty level and presentation of the problem with the conceptual level of the learners.

ITM can be used with learners of all age groups with suitable modification.

(I) For very young - use visual stimuli simple question give them clues to reduce cognitive strain.

(II) Older students - inquiry may be longer and student can access resource materials.

(III) More competent student - can arrange independent inquiry session for their friends.

Instructional (Direct) and Nurturant (Indirect) Effects:

It promotes strategies of inquiry and the values and attitudes that are essential to an inquiring mind.

- Process skills. (Observing, collecting and organizing data; identifying and controlling variables, formulating and testing hypothesis and explanation, inferring)
- Active learners.
- Verbal expression.
- Tolerance of ambiguity, persistence
- Logical thinking
- Attitude that all knowledge is tentative.

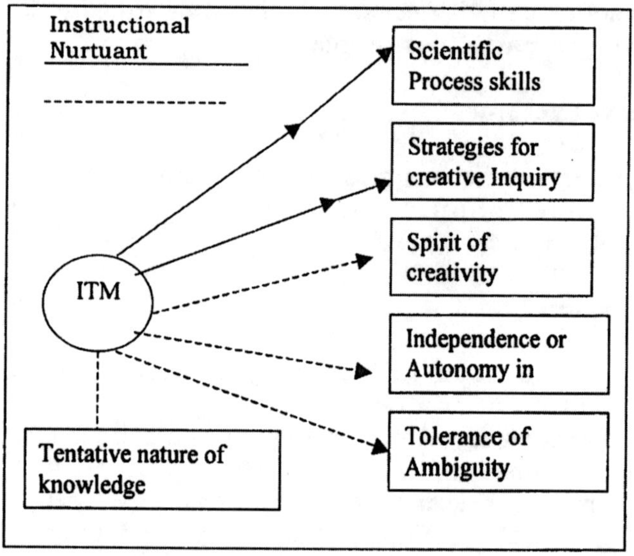

Instructional and Nurturant Effects of ITM

Limitations of Inquiry Training Model

(I) Model can help in developing explanation on the basis of previous knowledge.

It does not help in teaching, primary content for, e.g., new concepts and formula.

(II) If information about the puzzle is not presented in the form of a problem requiring explanation the student cannot arrive at generalization.

(III) It cannot be applied in puzzles where cause and effect relationship doesn't exist.

Class	:	XI
Subject	:	Biology
Topic	:	Phototropism
Duration	:	35 minutes.

Entry behavior

Students have knowledge that light (sun) plays an important role in the growth of plant.

General objective

Students will be able to know phototropism.

Model ITM

Method	:	Lecture cum demonstration.
Media	:	Potted plant, chart.
Approach	:	Inquiry approach.

Specific objectives

(1) Students will be able to explain phototropism.

(2) Students will be able to reason out the phototropism in plants.

Introduction

Good afternoon, students.

Today, we will study a topic with the help of activity. But before we proceed, I would like to give certain instructions to you. You have to thoroughly observe the activity, which we are going to perform.

You have to record the observation. Then based on your observation and changes in the activity you will ask certain questions. But you have to remember one thing, that your questions or inquiry should be asked in such a way that I can, give you answer in Yes or No, form.

Activity

- First teacher takes all the students to the school garden where sunlight is bright.
- Then teacher will select one potted plant of medium size. Keep the plant in bright sunlight.
- Then entire potted plant is covered with a box having only one opening.
- Keep the plant with box covering, as it is for 2-3 days in sunlight.
- Then after 2-3 days teacher again brings the students to garden to see the changes.
- Students observe the change that plant has bend towards one side.
- (Now, students have number of inquiries to be asked)
  Teacher asks what change you have observed.

Pupil

As the change is prominent so students will make out that bending of shoot has taken place towards one side.

(Now, they will ask questions to know why plant shoot has bend toward one side.)

It is due to darkness in box?

Teacher: No.

Pupil: Is it due to only one whole on the box?

Teacher: Yes.

Pupil: Is it due to air entering from one side has bent plant towards one side.

Teacher: No.

Pupil: Sunlight is also entering through the hole. Is it related to sunlight?

Teacher: Yes.

Pupil: Entry of sunlight from one side only has made bending of plant towards one side.

Teacher: Yes, very good.

The plant shoot has bend towards the source of light only. This is due to only a single hole in the box.

So, the phenomenon which involves the bending of plant shoot towards the source of light is phototropism. The term phototropism is consists of two words: -

Photo = light
Tropism = is related to movement.
So, movement of shoot towards the source of light.

As only one side of the plant shoot is exposed to the light so more growth has taken place on that side as compared to the unexposed portion. Due to this unequal growth of shoot the plant has bent on the one side i.e. the plant part, which is exposed, will carry out photosynthesis efficiently as compared to unexposed portion. So more growth of shoot will make bending of shoot towards that particular side. So, we can say that plants has tendency to bend towards the source of light. Now, same activity you can also check it at your home.

So, (today) with the help of phototropism activity we have learned that plants bent towards light source.

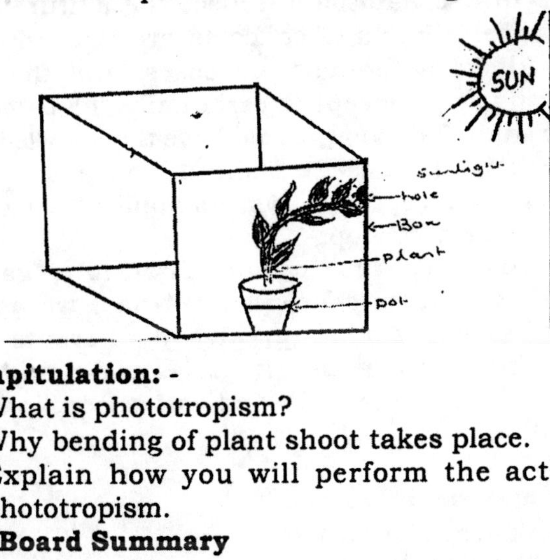

Recapitulation: -

(1) What is phototropism?
(2) Why bending of plant shoot takes place.
(3) Explain how you will perform the activity of phototropism.

Black – Board Summary

Date	Phototropism	XI Biology
Definition: - Phototropism means movement of plant towards the source of light.		

Home assignment: -

Perform an activity, by taking a box having two holes

on opposite side and keep the plant under the box in sunlight and make a record of observation.

CAM- Concept Attainment Model

CAM was developed by Jerome Bruner, Jacquline Goodnow and George Austin What is Concept? What is meant by knowing a concept?

Goals and Assumption

Bruner and his colleagues set out to study the thinking process called categorizing as the principle means by which a growing member of a society is socialized, for the categories that one is taught and comes to use habitually reflect the culture in which they arise. All sets of concepts are the product of the same kinds of thought processes, and the means of acquiring any concept is essentially the same.

To study CAM, one should have the knowledge of what concept is. In CAM we should have knowledge of particular concept and then its application to identify/ to recognize a concept

- Bruner, Austin and Goodnow, gave CAM. According to them concepts are "those words/symbols which represents a group/category of events processes etc having all elements". It's a generalized idea, which involves thinking process and varies from individual to individual.

There are two processes

(1) Concept formation

(2) Concept Attainment

All categorizing activities involve identifying and placing events into classes on the basis of using certain cues and ignoring others. According to Brunner categorizing activity has two components the act of **concept formation** and the act of **concept attainment**.

The distinction between concept formation and concept attainment, though subtle, is important because (1) the purpose and emphasis of these two forms of categorizing behavior are different. (2) The steps in these two procedures are same. (3) The two mental processes require different teaching processes.

Concept formation may have groups of examples and many concepts; concept Attainment has one concept.

Concept Attainment teaching

Requirements are minimal – an array of instances or examples that are alike in some ways and different in other. At each encounter a person formulates hypothesis and reformulates a hypothesis about the concept. Each instance or example provides potential information about the characteristics and attribute values of the concept.

Bruner sees any concept as having 5 elements.

(1) Name (2) Examples (positive and negative) (3) Attributes (essential and nonessential) (4) Attribute values (5) Rule.

Understanding a concept means knowing all the elements of the concept.

1. There should be a name of concept, i.e., concepts are those words which have some name. example fruit, dog, tree etc. The name may vary according to the concept.

- fruit is a concept

2. There should be examples of the concept i.e. it is a group of something concept isn't a single word. It is based on symbols/words.

There are 2 types of examples.

Positive examples are those, which represents directly the particular concept having all the essential characters. While negative examples are those, which have only half-essential characters? Every concept has both positive and negative examples.

Example Fruits.

(1) There is a name.

(2) Apples, oranges, pears, watermelon positive all are edible fruits.

They all develop by ripening of ovary. Fruits have common character's Apples and Pears the other two are distinctly different.

(3) Each concept has some attributes. An attribute is a property or character of an object, which differentiates it from the other in terms of colour, texture, size, number of parts, position and sound etc.

The characters can be classified as:

(a) Essential

(b) Non Essential

Fruits may be fleshy/dry, seed enclosing/sweet or sour edible/not edible.

Cost is non essential and fluctuating on demand and supply.

(4) Each concept has attribute value.

Example color is attribute, different range of colours.

Apple can be green, yellow, red similarly shape is an attribute.

(5) Each concept has rule/definition. Definition is on the basis of synthesis and thus arrives from summary it involves analysis which is highest level of cognitive Domain.

Example Apple is a concept.
Tree is a concept
Living things is a concept.
Triangle.

The rule clearly states the nature of the concept by indicating all the essential attributes.

- The distinguishing attributes and their unique value range are called **criterial attributes**. If any one criterial attribute is missing from an object that object is example of different concept.

Types of concept

1. *Concrete Concept*: There are concepts, which exist, can be proved, and number of examples can be given. E.g. flower plant etc.

2. *Abstract Concept*: Concepts, which can't be proved, have number existence and number of examples can be an abstract concept. Example life, emotion, pain, pleasures.

3. *Secondary concept*: - Concepts where number of primary.

Concepts are present they are complex concept, e.g. tissue, organ etc. primary concept – where a single clear concept is given.

According to Bruner concepts are of 3 types.

1. **Conjunctive Concept**: A concept in which more than one attribute is present. I related with **and** e.g. flower is a modified shoot of a plant **and** a reproductive organ of plant.

2. **Disjunctive Concept**: Concept having and attributes in which one is present or absent. Its related with **or** e.g. Oxidation is either removal of H_2/or addition of O_2.

3. **Relational Concept**: Concept having all social relations like mother – father etc.

Thinking strategies involved in CAM

In addition to attaining (1) a particular concept, a second purpose of the CAM is to acquaint students with the conceptualizing process itself. (2) This includes understanding the relationships among data examples. (3) attributes (4) and concepts (5) and the thinking patterns that are used to attain the concept.

An *ideal strategy* is one that is most efficient in attaining the concept but has the least amount of cognitive strain resulting from memory overload, ambiguity and so on.

Bruner distinguishes between the *two learning conditions* of *selection* and *reception.*

In *selection* conditions, the examples are not marked yes or no. An individual selects one and inquires whether it is yes or no.

In *reception* condition, the teacher presents the example in a prearranged order labeling them yes or no.

In schools reception condition is most common.

Selection thinking Strategies

Bruner and his associates have identified six strategies – four selection strategies and two reception strategies.

1. Simultaneous scanning
2. Successive scanning
3. Conservative focusing
4. Focus Gambling

Strategies for Searching

	Attribute(s)	**Concept(s)**
Many	Conservative focusing	Simultaneous scanning
One at a time	Focus gambling	Successive scanning

Simultaneous

(1) Attributes or concept hypothesis is analyzed at a time.

(2) Successive scanning: Number of attributes and hypothesis are formed/held at a time.

(3) Conservative focusing: Its based on the attributes of a concept Ist find positive instance than (individual attribute is valueable). One attribute at a time is chosen.

(4) Focus gamblers: Use a positive instance as a focus and change one or more attribute at a time.

Reception thinking

The two reception strategies are:

1. Wholist (like focusing)
2. Partist (like scanning)

1. Wholist: Wholist strategy takes first positive instance of the concept and use it in to as a guide. Comparing all attributes of first one with others.

1st instance becomes concept hypothesis.

2. Partist: The choice of hypothesis is based on only part of the initial example. If the initial hypothesis is not confirmed the partist refers to all previous instances and changes the hypothesis.

Wholist strategy is regarded as the ideal selection strategy – one that minimizes strain and maximizes performance.

CAM

Hydrocarbons	*Yes*	*No*
	H	Ca
	O	Mg
	C	Cd
	S	Na
	N	
	X	K

Unlabelled CH_4
Benzene Ketone
Ethane Acetone
Propane
Methanol

VII	*Yes*	*No*	
Useful Animals	Cow	Scorpion	Unlabelled
	Buffalo	Snake	Bees
	Goat	Cockroach	Vasp
	Earthworm	Termite	Frog
	Silk worm	Mosquitoes	Lizard
			Oysters.
Wild Animals	Positive	Negative	Unlabelled.
	Lion Elephant	Dog Cat	Giraffe Turtle
	Wolf	Squirrel	Fish
	Fox	Parrot	Python
	Owl		Dear
			Wild Ass
Beverages	Tea	Apple	Unlabelled
	Coco	Bread	Bhelpuri
	Coffee	Biscuits	Chholle
	Coconut	Chutney	Fanta
			Mirinda

Model of Teaching

The reception model is more direct in teaching students the elements of a concept and their use in concept attainment.

Syntax:

1. **Phase one** involves presenting data to the learner.

Each unit of data is a separate example or non-example of the concept. The data may be events, people, objects, stories, pictures or any other discernable unit.

Students are informed there is one idea that all positive examples have in common their task is to develop hypothesis about the concept.

The instances are presented in a prearranged order and are labeled 'yes' or 'no'.

Learners are asked to compare and justify the attributes of different examples.

Finally they are asked to name their concept and state the rule or definition of the concept according to its essential attributes.

With some concepts students may not know the name, which can be provided when the concept is confirmed.

2. **Phase two**: The student test their attainment of the concept, first by correctly identifying additional unlabeled examples of the concept and then by generating their own examples.

After this teacher confirms or disconfirms their hypothesis revising the choice of concept or attribute as necessary.

3. **In Phase three**: Students begin to analyze the strategies by which they attain concepts.

Gradually students can compare the effectiveness of different strategies.

2. Social System

1. Teacher chooses the concept.
2. Selects and organizes the material into positive and negative examples.
3. Sequences the examples.

The teacher will have to select a concept and by referring text and other books will have to frame positive and negative examples.

Teacher also supplies additional examples as needed.

Three major functions of teacher are to

1. Record

2. Prompt (cue)
3. Present additional information.

3. Principles of Reaction

During the flow of the lesson the teacher wants to be supportive.

In the later phase the teacher wishes to turn the student attention towards analysis, of their concepts and their thinking strategy.

The teacher should encourage analysis of the merit of various strategies.

4. Support System Concept attainments lessons require material that has been designed so that concepts are embedded in the material with positive and negative examples.

5. Application

1. The use of the model determines the shape of particular learning activities. Participation is more important.
2. CAM may be used with all ages and grades levels.
3. In secondary selection strategy and unorganized strategy are important and useful.
4. CAM is excellent evaluation tool teachers can quickly know the depth of student understanding and reinforce their previous knowledge.
5. The model can also be useful in opening up a new conceptual area by initiating a sequence of individual or group inquiries.
6. If a concept is controversial the teacher can present several interpretations of it which the students can debate.

6. Instructional and Nurturant Effects

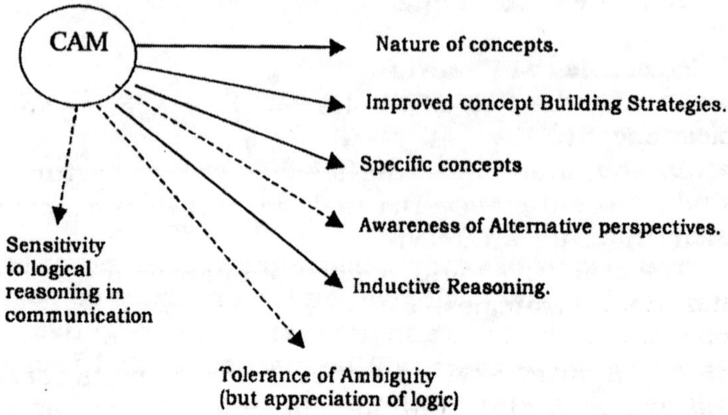

Class: XI **Period:**
Subject: Biology **Time:**

Topic: True Coelomates

Type of Model : - ROCAM.

Education Objectives

1. Student will be able to identify the true coelomates.
2. Student will be able to write the characteristics of coelomates.
3. Student will be able to differentiate coelomates from acoelomates.

Name of the concept

True coelomates.

Medium of the concept

Pictures.

Essential attributes

1. They are triploblastic animals.
2. They have 2 body cavities – digestive and coelomic cavity.
3. This cavity is surrounded by mesodermal peritoneum.

Non-essential attributes

1. They have bilateral symmetry.
2. They have vertebral column.

3. They may be terrestrial.
4. Cavity is formed by splitting of mesoderm.

Rule

Coelomates are triploblastic animals who have coelome as the body cavity. This cavity is formed by mesoderm and is surrounded by mesodermal peritoneum. They start from annelids to mammals.

Introduction

Today we will study a new topic in a different joyful manner. Initially I will give you few examples as positive examples of the topic and few examples as negative ones. Based on these there will be discussion and then you will have to answer some of my question. Also you will be preparing a work sheet for yourself.

Syntax

Phase – 1: Presentation of data

Teacher shows them the pictures of following animals and labels them as positive and negative.

Positive	*Negative*
Earth warm	Tape worm
Oyster	Amoeba/paramoecium
Star fish	Sponges
Prawn	Liver fluke
Mammal	Hydra
Amphioxus/Testuda	Ascaris

Worksheet

Positive	*Negative*	*Hypothesis*	*Reason.*
Earth worm	Tape worm	Perhaps you are talking about worms.	Because both, e.g., are representing worms.
Oyster	Paramoecium	Perhaps you are talking about economically useful animals.	Because positive, e.g., 1 & 2 represent it.
Star fish	Sponges	Perhaps you are talking of some other group of animals.	Because negative, e.g., is also an economically useful one.
Prawn	Liver fluke	Perhaps you are talking about higher animals.	Because all positive e.g., are from higher hierarchy and negative are from lower hierarchy.
Mammal	Hydra	Perhaps you are talking about true coelome.	Because positive, e.g., show this character.
Testudo	Ascaris	Yes, you are talking about coelomates.	-

Student will look at the diagram and prepare this worksheet and formulate the hypothesis.

Phase -II. Testing the concept attainment

Teacher: - Let's see if the idea you guessed as my concept is correct by testing it. I will give you some examples and you tell me if they are yes/no. Teacher gives following examples.

Leech, cockroach, paramoecium, jellyfish, scorpion, coral.

Student: - Classify them as

positive	*negative*
Leech	Paramoecium/amoeba
Cockroach	Jelly fish
Scorpion	coral

Teacher: Well you have done it correctly. Now each of you gives atleast one positive example.

Student: Rabbit, sparrow, snake, fish, Toad, frog, seaurchin, octopus, locust etc.

Teacher: Very nice.

Teacher tests by asking: can you name the concept? Can you tell the peculiarities of this group of animals? Then teacher tells the rule.

Phase III: Analyzing thinking strategy

Teacher asks following as:

1. What did the first example reveal to you?
2. Did you change your mind at any example? If yes, then at which example did you do this and why?
3. Which example confirmed your hypothesis?

Social System

Role of teacher

Teacher will collect the e.g., sequence them and present them in proper order. She will keep the record of hypothesis and provide calls. Finally she will give additional information about the types of true coelome and different between true, pseudo and acoelomate.

Role of student

They will formulate the hypothesis, make worksheet and check their thinking strategy.

Principles of Reaction

Teacher will support the hypothesis formulated by student and help them to attain right concept.

Support system

Pictures XIth standard Textbook, Invertebrate zoology by P.S. Verma.

Instructional effects

Students have understood that coelomates start from group annelida. They have also understood that these organisms have a body cavity formed by mesoderm.

Nurturant Effects

Student will have developed awareness about various alternatives like acoelomates, pseudocoelomates.

Also tolerance and respect towards others ideas.

SPONGE

HYDRA

PARAMOECIUM

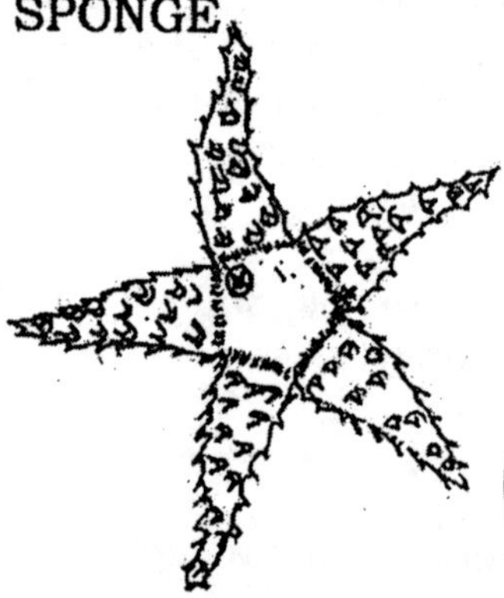

STAR FISH

TAPE WORM

SCALY ANT EATER

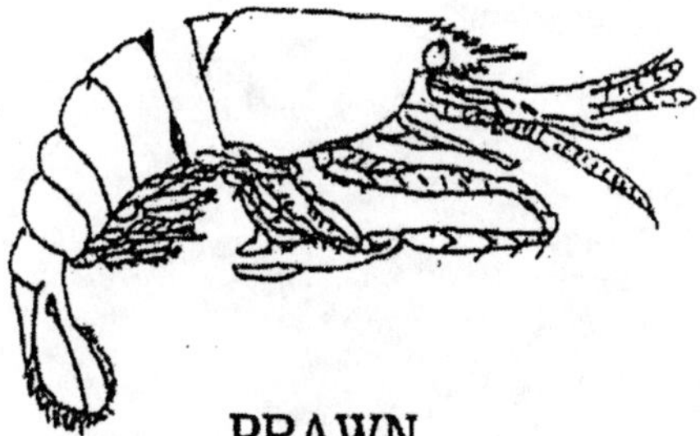

PRAWN

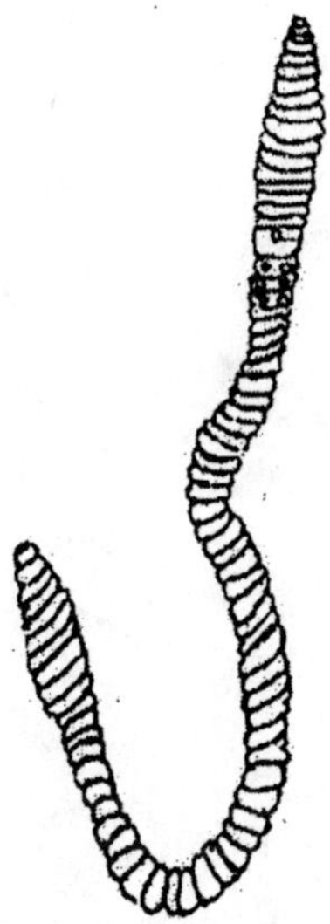

EARTHWORM

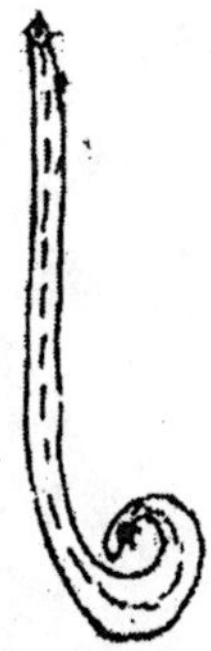

ASCARIS

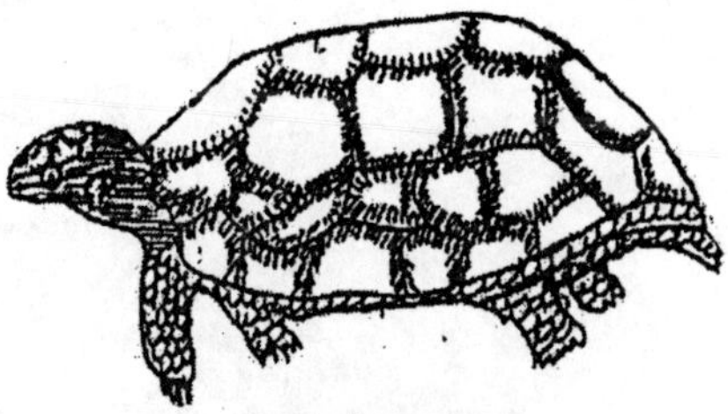

TESTUDO

OYSTER

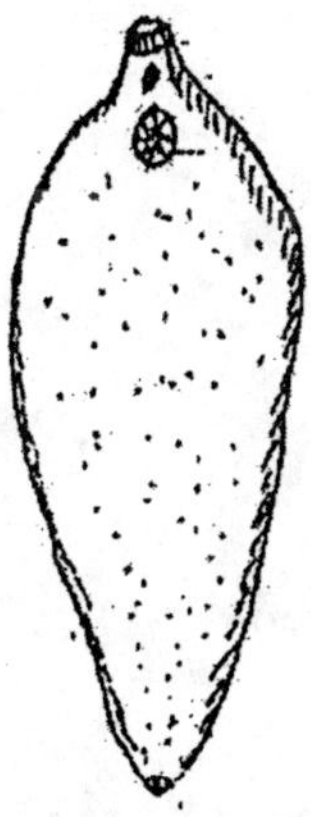

LIVER FLUKE

8
Laboratory

Aims and objectives of biology cannot be achieved without laboratory. There should be no distinction in practical and theoretical work in fact both should complement each other. Objectives of laboratory work learning outcomes of laboratory experience.

(i) Awakening and maintenance of curiosity in the environment.

(ii) Illustration and verification of abstract scientific ideas.

(iii) Development of skills, such as, measurement, accuracy, use of microscope etc.

(iv) Using it as an educational device for answering questions experimentally thereby providing training in scientific methods.

(v) Prepare students for higher studies and science careers.

(vi) To develop habit of doing independent work among students.

(vii) Avoid memorizing subject.

(viii) Develop habit of reasoning.

(ix) Have a clear understanding of concept.

(x) Improve observation and critical thinking.

Types of laboratory activities.

1. Verification
2. Exploratory
3. Inductive
4. Deductive
5. Psychomotor
6. Problem solving.

1. Verification: These activities are used to verify major concepts, events and phenomena.

2. Exploratory: Students are encouraged to investigate through open-ended problems it is used to find new information and scientific relationship.

3. Inductive: Questions are posed to students and they are guided to discover a relationship or a concept on their own.

Inductive activities helps in seeing relationships and realizing facts, leading towards generalization.

4. Deductive: It is based on general to specific maxim student apply previous knowledge in explaining facts and principles.

5. Psychomotor: Skill development: - Students are given the opportunity to practice requisite psychomotor skills.

6. Problem Solving: Students solve scientific problems and formulate answers. Students learn to attack the problems from various levels and develop the skill of solving the problem.

Preparing Students for laboratory experience

Pre Laboratory Discussion

Before starting laboratory work make clear.

1. Theory of the practical.
2. What to find?
3. Why to find?
4. How to find?
5. Where to find?

} Also importance of that practical

Any other special instruction required while teaching biology practical should be given.

(i) **Objectives of experiment**: The objective of experiment should be clear to student then only they can proceed in right direction.

(ii) **Procedure**: Teacher and student discuss the procedure.

(iii) **Requirements**: What are the chemicals?

What are the apparatus?
Specifically needed for the experiment.
How to set/arrange the apparatus?
How to use the apparatus?

(iv) **Precaution**: It is teacher's responsibility to prevent any kind of accident in the laboratory, clear and precise instructions should be given. Proper instructions and direction will lead to success of experiment.

Giving Directions

In some schools, card system is practiced for giving guidance to pupils every student is given a card containing instructions about the experiment, students have to perform.

- The use of cards saves time.
- The card should give both concise and precise information.
- Main purpose of experiment should be made clear. The card of 6" X 4" are used.

The card has following information.

(i) Number of experiment.
(ii) Purpose of experiment.
(iii) Method/Procedure to be adopted.
(iv) Precautions.
(v) Method of tabulating result.
(vi) Some questions can be given which help in developing a thinking process that will take the student closer to the conclusion of the experiment.
(vii) Conclusion.

One must cater to the needs to

1. Fast learner – fast will finish and trouble
2. Average learner and - will need few and directions.
3. Slow learner – will need lot of guidance.

Post Laboratory Discussion

Teacher should know how students conduct experiment for this post laboratory discussion is needed.

(i) **Observation**: - Although the experiment is same the observations may vary from individual to individual.

This may be due to:

- The way of doing the experiment.
- Previous experience.
- Sometimes due to apparatus.
- Individual differences.

So, the group has to discuss the reason of getting different observations.

(ii) Generalization: - On the basis of the correct observations group has to arrive at conclusion and they will generalize it.

(ii) Reasons of failure

Although we have adopted scientific procedure but failure is quite possible. Therefore as a science student everyone is supposed to know the reason of failure.

The reasons may be:

- Outdated Chemicals.
- Contaminated apparatus.
- Human mistake.
- Wrong Procedure.
- Errors in Interpretation.
- Physical factors like temperature light humidity.

Safety Measures in Laboratory

It is important to train students in the use and practice of safety rules and use of first aid etc.

Common accidents and their Remedies

Accident	*Remedies*
Burn.	
a) By Dry heat	Use Burnol and sarson oil.
b) Acid Burn	Wash it with H_2O or $NaHCO_3$ and finally Tannic acid.
c) Alkali Burn	Wash it with 1% of CH_3COOH or lime water.
d) Phosphorous burn	Treat with $AGNO_3$.

Cut.	
a) Minor cut	Allow it to bleed for a few second apply sprit or detol and cover with Handyplast.
b) Deep cut	Try to stop bleeding by applying pressure, Apply $FeCl_3$.
Eye Accident	
a) Acid in Eye	Wash the eye with water, followed by 1% Na_2CO_3.
b) Alkali in Eye	Wash the eye with water followed by 1% Boric acid.
c) Foreign particles in Eye	Do not rub the eye. Remove the particle by means of soft cloth.
Poison	
a) Acid	Dilute by drinking water or milk of magnesia.
b) Caustic Alkalides	Dilute by drinking water or lemon juice.
c) Mercury compounds.	Immediately give an emetic or Zinc Sulphate.
Inhalation of Gases Like SO_2, NO_2	Remove the victim to the open air, loosen the clothes. Give dilute vapours of NH_3 or gargle with $NaHCO_3$.

First Aid Kit

Accidents usually occur in laboratory. So it is important to have first Aid kit in the laboratory.

- Laboratory should be kept in good condition.
- Well organized.
- Every thing should be properly labeled.

In First aid box following things should be there.

1. Bandages
2. Cotton
3. Detol
4. Scissors
5. Dropper
6. Safety pins
7. Aspirin
8. Acetic Acid
9. Adhesive tape
10. Burnol
11. Castor oil
12. Mustard oil
13. Ether
14. Lime water

First aid is the immediate care given to a person who has been injured or has suddenly fallen ill.

First aid box should always be in reach in the laboratory to look after the victim.

Aim of first Aid

-To preserve life.

-To prevent worsening of condition.

-To promote recovery.

Heavy Bleeding

-Wash the wound with water and soap.

-Apply A+ meditex Antiseptic cream on the dressing

-Place the dressing on the wound.

-Apply elastic plaster on the wound.

A proper training in the use of first aid is given to the students so that the student can apply the right medicine in case of certain accident even when teacher is not there.

Planning, Organization and Maintenance of Biology Laboratory

The laboratory should be well planned and properly equipped.

A good laboratory should be:

(i) Spacious – So that students can work and move easily.

(ii) Quite and conducive for hard work. Should have fresh air, temp, ventilation, light and heat.

(iii) Flexible: for effective teaching and demonstrations.

(iv) Must permit teachers. Supervision.

(v) Must have storage space for chemicals and equipments.

(vi) Must have water, gas and electric points.

(vii) Emergency exit.

Planning for Infrastructure

We have to consider some points before making a biology laboratory.

1. The number of pupil working at a time.
2. Minimum space required for each pupil.
3. Place for storage.
4. Complete teacher supervision.
5. Each student can see the demonstration.
6. Blackboard is visible to each student.
7. Master switches for water, gas and electricity.
8. Available Finance.

Things to consider while constructing laboratory

1) **Location**: Preferable located at the ground floor away from playground.

2) **Flexibility**: Suitable for different types of activities science club.

3) **Furniture**: Should be portable and adaptable Almirah with glass panel.

4) **Ventilation**: Proper ventilation should be provided Exhaust fan must be provided.

5) **Supervision**: The class should be in visual control of teacher.

6) **Safety**: Master controls and first aid should be readily available.

7) **Wet Bench Area**: Separate area for aquarium preparation and experiments needing fresh plant material.

8) **Lighting**: Provision for natural light should be there.

9) **Pupil Working Area**: Sufficient space, Acid resistant table, stool, water supply, bookshelf, wall clock, and drainage sink.

10) **Teacher Working Area**: Demonstration table with a Blackboard. 6′ × 3 ½ × 3′ acid proof paint with sink, gas and water connection. A fixed screen for projections, films and diagrams Black Board 10′ × 4′ dark green or brown (UNESCO).

11) **Preparation Area**: Preparation room equipped with all services like light, gas, electric points, waste disposal shelving and cupboards.

12) **Storage Room**: Storage space for prepared materials, equipment, apparatus, charts, and models, audio visual aids, almirah, racks and sink.

13) **Reference Room**: Consult books.

14) **Botanical Garden and Living Animal**: Green house, froggery.

15) **Museum and Herbarium**: Almirahs, dry exhibits, leaves roots, fish, snakes, insects etc.

16) **Aquarium**: Permanent place for aquarium should be there.

17) **Display Board**: Arouse curiosity and stimulate interests and raise questions.

18) **Fire Extinguisher**: - In bio laboratory there is less chance of fire. It should have one fire extinguisher and one fire blanket.

Planning for Equipments and Apparatus

Procuring of adequate and right type of apparatus is most important aspect of laboratory.

Planning: -

Requirement

1) Apparatus for laboratory work.
2) Apparatus for demonstration.
3) Apparatus for general use.

While determining the quantity of apparatus to be purchased, we should keep the following points in mind.

1) Finance.
2) Demonstration and laboratory work.
3) Storage space available.
4) Number of students.

Following articles and apparatus are necessary.

1) Microscope
2) Slides
3) Test tubes
4) Test tube holders
5) Jar
6) Cover slips
7) Dropper
8) Stains
9) Bottles
10) Hotplate
11) Oven
12) Spoon
13) Knife
14) Blade
15) Burrette
16) Pipettes
17) Spirit lamp
18) Balance
19) Dissection Microscope
20) Working Model
21) Projector

Organization

After planning organization is the 2nd stage.

Organization of laboratory can be divided into 2 parts.

1. Administration of laboratory.
2. Arrangement of apparatus.

(i) **Administration of laboratory**: It should be under the supervision of laboratory attendant.

- Person having B.Sc.
- Work as laboratory storekeeper-cum-laboratory assistant.
- Minimum qualification – Matriculation.

Cards should be made for each experiment cards of do's and don't should be prepared.

(ii) **Arrangement of apparatus**

- Apparatus should be arranged in glass almirah's
- Each and every item should be easily located.
- Apparatus should be arranged topic wise or alphabetically.
- Dangerous and costly chemicals should be stored separately.
- List of chemicals and articles should be pasted on almirah.
- Poisonous chemical should be kept in lock and key.

Entry of Apparatus in the Stock Register

Articles received should be checked properly and entered.

We can enter them in

1. Permanent Stock Register – Articles.
2. Breakable Stock Register – Glassware's
3. Consumable Stock Register – Chemicals

A separate requirement register should be maintained by teacher to note down the requirement. He she should consult register at the time of purchase.

Maintenance

"Maintaining something is 100 times difficult task then developing, constructing something.

We can divide the maintenance into two parts.

1. Maintenance of Laboratory.
2. Maintenance of Apparatus.

1. **Maintenance of Laboratory**
   - White washing
   - Regular repair

2. **Maintenance of Apparatus**
   - Equipments and apparatus should be cleaned properly.
   - Metal and woody articles should be polished.
   - Broken articles should be replaced immediately.
   - A sheet of laboratory instruction should be hung in the laboratory and the student should be asked to follow it strictly.

Assessment of laboratory work

Evaluation is the process to check or measure the extent of change in behavior.

Evaluation is continuous and comprehensive process.

Purpose of Evaluation

1. Assesses the extent of learning.
2. Teacher gets the feedback about learning gaps in student knowledge.
3. Teacher gets feedback about the quality of teaching.
4. Student get opportunity to show their worth.
5. It serves as a tool for screening students for special purpose.

Assessment of Laboratory Work

Taradevi Report. Suggested following pattern Evaluation in science.

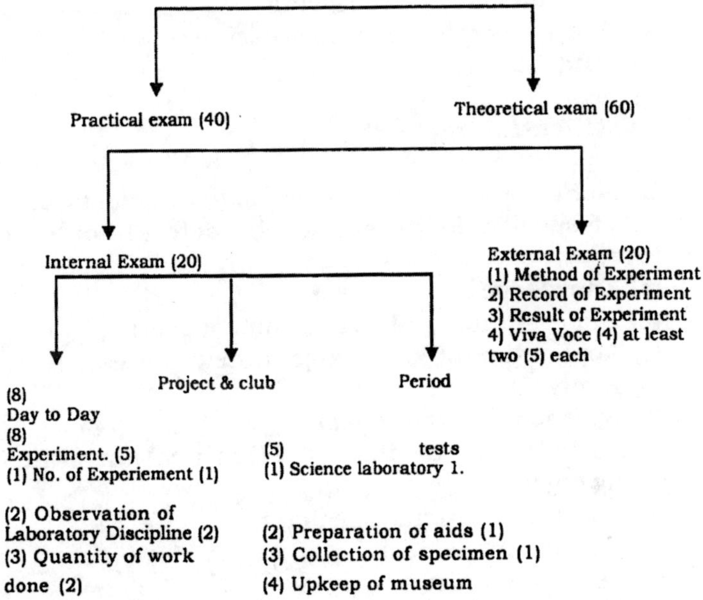

Assessment of laboratory work could be done with various tests.

(a) Manipulative test	—	50%
(b) Identification test	—	25%
(c) Observation of process skill.	—	10%
d) Assessment of affect level outcomes.	—	10%
(e) Viva voce and Record	—	5%

A. Manipulative and Observation Test

(i) Use of Microscope.
(ii) Section cutting.
(iii) Preparation of permanent slides.
(iv) Manipulating the objectives.
(v) Titration.
(vi) Dissection.

Process skills have to be evaluated by

1. Way of Processing
2. Clarity of Processing
3. Confidence in Processing
4. Proper sequence in Processing
5. End Result.

B. Identification test

Students have to identify biological objects on the bases of specific features and characters. For it they require.

(a) Knowledge about object.
(b) Understanding about various aspects.
(c) Application of knowledge in new context.
(d) Analysis of the object.
(e) Synthesis of the object.

A student has to develop identification skill for following objects.

(a) Plant and animal specimen.
(b) Permanent slides.
(c) Living organism.
(d) Various apparatus.
(e) Various parts of organism.

Spoting – student identify, draw and write comment within given period.

C. Affect Level Development Test

Aim of education is integrated development of Head, Heart and Hand.

We have to evaluate the students on the following basis.

(a) Dealing with experimental organism.
(b) Enthusiasm in doing experiment.
(c) Spirit of group work.
(d) Behavior with other students in laboratory.
(e) Sensitivity towards the laboratory.
(f) Regularity.
(g) Punctuality.

(h) Dedication towards the lab and lab work.
(i) Responsibility for laboratory work.
(j) Scientific temper.

We can evaluate the affect level development of student by using any of the following technique.

(a) Anecdotal Record
(b) Tape recording
(c) Situation Evaluation.
(d) Children work project.
(e) Teachers observation.

D. Viva -Voce

Viva holds important place in assessment of laboratory work. Viva is important in assessment because.

(a) Some experiment. may result into failure without any fault. On the basis of viva teacher can allot marks.

(b) It will give authenticity of the experiment performed by the student.

(c) How much students have conceptualized?

d) The aim and objective of experiment has been achieved or not.

Through viva we can evaluate the students.

(a) Scientific knowledge.
(b) Scientific attitude
(c) Critical thinking ability

E. Record Book

Record book should also hold some weight. For preparation and maintenance of the record following things should be kept in mind.

(a) Regularity in preparing the record book.
(b) Sensitivity towards the record book.
(c) Accuracy in diagrams and calculations.
(d) Originality of work.
(e) Interest of the students.

Through Evaluation of Record Book

We can know: -

(a) Drawing skills.
(b) Mathematical calculation skill.
(c) Presentation skill.

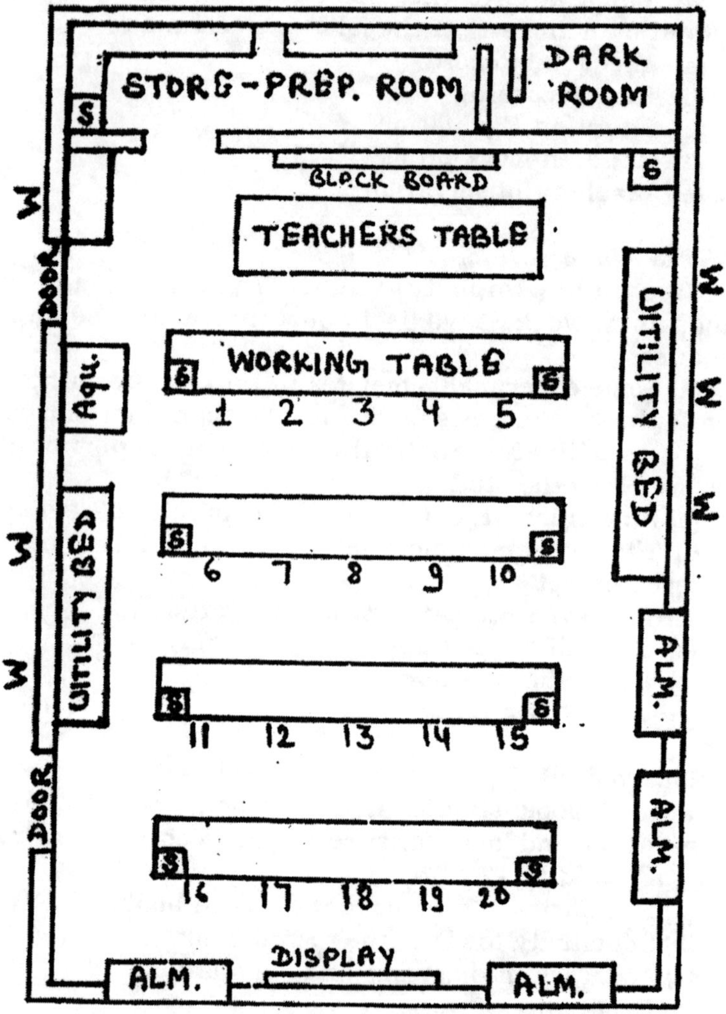

Picture 10. All purpose science laboratory

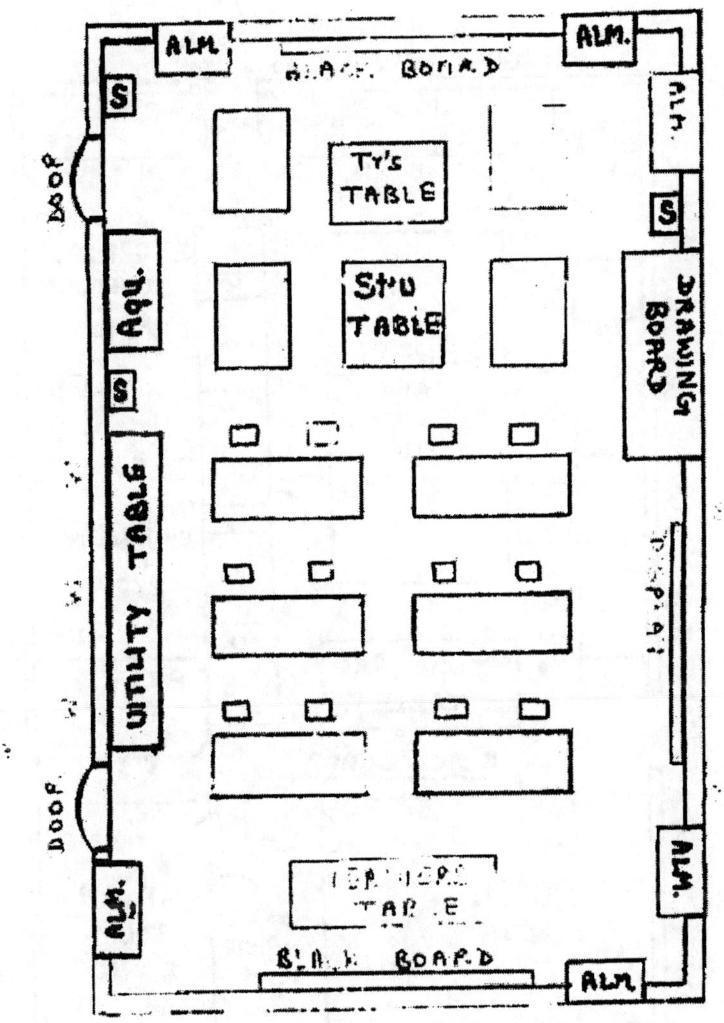

Picture 11. Lecture – Room – Cum - Laboratory

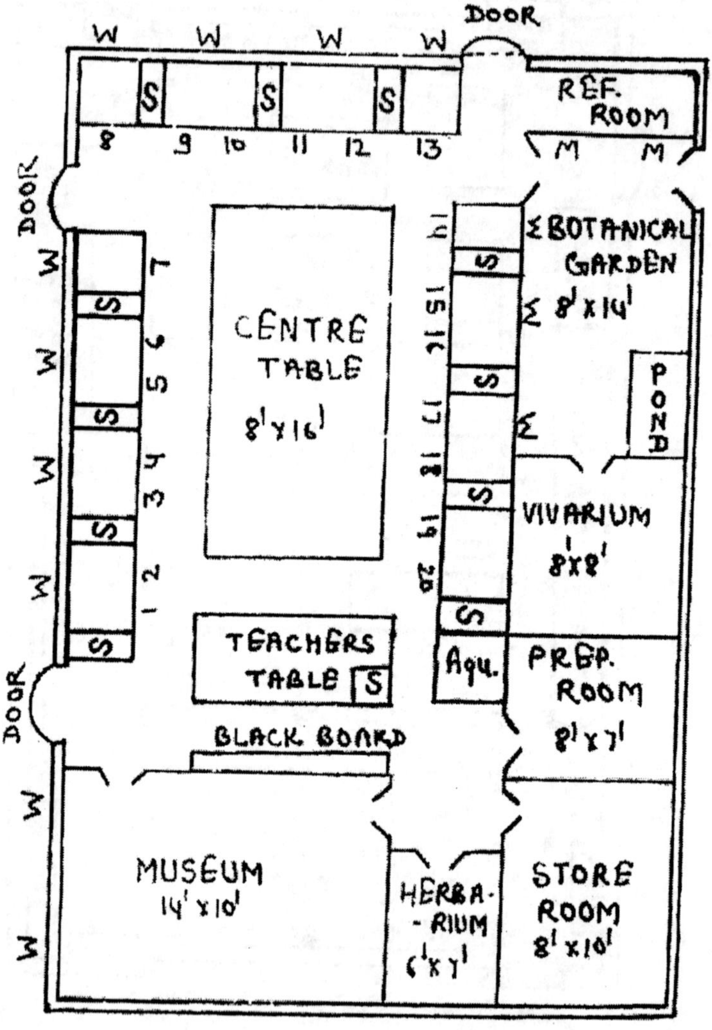

Picture 12. Ideal biology laboratory

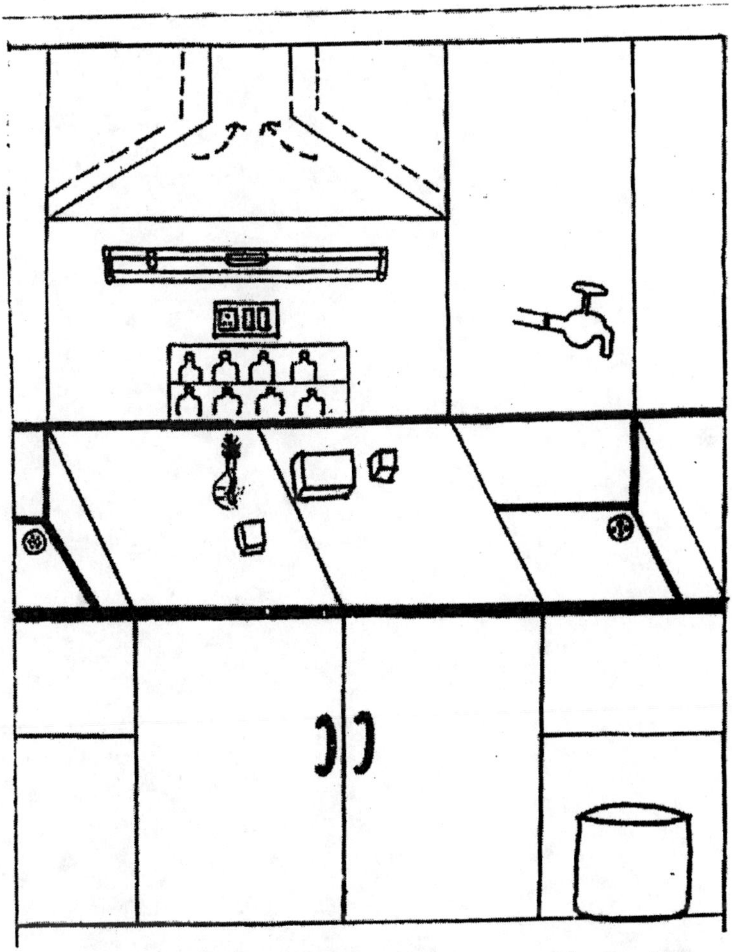

Picture 13. Ideal Biology Working Table for Two Students

(DBT - 1992)

9
Curriculum Organisation

It has been said that "Curriculum is the soul of the process of education. It is the heart of the educational institution and mind of the course and all that only goes with it."

The word curriculum in derived from a Latin word 'currere,' which means 'to run'. So, "the curriculum means a course to be run for reaching a certain goal." This definition does not inform us enough specifically and intelligently. Historically speaking, it meant clarified selections made from the accumulated knowledge into separate subjects, or disciplines to be taught to students. From there arose other specialized curriculums like business curriculum and the college preparatory curriculum etc. in U.S.A. Other activities or learning experience considered important by the school were first of all called extra-curricular and later on the term co-curricular came into vague. In fact the term curriculum has a rich past in itself in an interesting subject of study.

According to Cunningham, "Curriculum is the tool in the hands of the artist (the teacher) to mould his material (the pupils) according to his ideal (aims and objectives) in his studies (the school)."

An important definition of curriculum states the role and characteristics of a curriculum, i.e., "The requisite content of knowledge arranged systematically for progressive acquisition; the total living to the child so far as the school can influence it or should take responsibility for developing it. The specialized environment deliberately arranged for directing the interests and abilities of children towards effective participation in the life of the community and the nation; concerned with helping children, enrich their own lives and contribute to the improvement of the society through the acquisition of useful information's, skills and attitudes. The teaming experiences which children and youth have under the direction of school; the sequence of potential experience set up in the school. The purpose of disciplining children and youth in group; ways of thinking and acting; the continuous activity of the individual interacting with the environmental factors about his, learning or changes in behavior that occur in the chain of series of experiencing. The systematic arrangement of courses designed to meet the needs of a pupil or a group of pupils; the complete school environment involving all the courses, activities, readings and associations furnished to the pupils in the guidance of the school; all the learning experiences provided by the school, class study, health, recreation services and guidance services, social inheritance organized for its rapid assimilation by immature minds. The means to attain the aims of education, viz., the complete manhood for the attainment of a new life; and all the experience which take place under the sponsorship of the school.

According to the Secondary Education Commission's Report, 'Curriculum is much more than the boundaries by the academic subjects taught traditionally.' 'It should include totality of experiences that pupil receives through the manifold activities that go on in the school, in the classroom, library, laboratory, workshop, playgrounds and in the numerous informed contents between teachers and pupils. In this sense, the whole life of the school becomes the curriculum and helps in the evolution of balanced personality.

According to Good,f "A general overall plan of the content or specific materials of instructions that the school should offer the student by way of qualifying him for graduation or certification for entrance into a professional or a vocational field."

According to Crow and Crow, "Curriculum includes all learners experience in or outside the school that are included in a programme which has been devised to help him develop mentally, physically, socially, emotionally, spiritually and morally."

According to Munroe, "Curriculum embodies all the experiences which are utilized by the school to attain the aims of education.

According to Marshall C. Jameson and W.M. Vemod Hider – As interpreted, "education must consist of meaningful and purposeful experiences if it is to have permanent usefulness. Curriculum is viewed almost synonymously with the term "education". When the experiences are those for which the school accepts responsibility. There curriculum experiences are organized and guided in order that acceptable objectives and needs of children are met the needs being social, emotional, intellectual and physical."

Modern Concepts of Curriculum

Earlier the major aim of education was the acquisition of a fund of information.

But now education in regarded as a dynamic process and so the aims and objectives have changed. It is not merely the covers of study but is the sum – total of the experiences of the pupils that he receives through the various activities that go on in the school, in the classroom, in the laboratory, in the workshop, in the playground and in the numerous informal contacts between the teacher and the pupils. It is much more than the subject matter as it is traditionally conceived.

So, curriculum is an evolving concept, i.e., it is always in the making, being more in the nature of a process than a finished product. It informs us what to teach before we can consider methods and approaches to teaching and the age at which the various ideas are to be introduced.

According to Smith, Stanley and Shores, there are four significant dimensions essentially to be considered when one talks of curriculum development. They are the determination of educational directions, the choice of principles and procedures for selecting and ordering the potential experiences comprising the instructions programme, the selection of a pattern of curriculum organization and the determination of principles and procedures by which changes in the curriculum can be made.

Aside from the acquisition of information, which is the dominating aim, the teaching of biology should also provide for the development of scientific attitudes, interests, skills etc. in order to affect the maximum growth on the part of the learner. Since curriculum is the totality of experiences of a child, and the experiences of each child are different from other, so the curriculum will be different for each student in the school.

Variables which affect Curriculum

As a curriculum does not exist in isolation. It comes about as a resultant of many variables having varying degrees of mutual interaction, which impinge on it. Though the curriculum in the case of the whole educational enterprise, it in likely to be affected by the other process or aspects of education.

These variables are:

Teacher: Teacher is the major factor in the curriculum because teacher is a person who is in direct contact with the students and he is only going to deal with curriculum. Only teacher will be having the comprehensive knowledge about the interests, attitude, need, and intelligence level of the student.

Research: Research is an important aspect in designing the curriculum. As in this modern world knowledge is doubling after every 5 years, So for introducing, recent innovation and updating the previous knowledge research is very helpful.

Availability of Expert Guidance and Advice:

Curriculum designing is not one man job. It requires the help of different subject experts in deciding the objectives, principles and the subject matter. So the effective curriculum can be designed with the guidance and advice of the different field expert.

Pupils: Basically curriculum is designed for the pupils. So it should take into consideration the age, level, interest, need, attitude of the pupils. If curriculum satisfied all these necessities of pupils, then only it can successfully work out in the school.

Supervision and Administration: This factor is important in curriculum organization to check whether the curriculum is following the right direction or not. If it getting modified according to the recent changes.

Examination and Evaluation: This factor plays an important role to check whether the pre-determined goals on which all the activities of the curriculum are based are achieved or not. This factor helps in diagnosing the learning difficulty in present curriculum and to modify it according to the levels of the student.

Instruction and Illustrative material: While designing the curriculum the care should be taken it is designed in comprehensive manner. It should include more illustrating materials, so, that it is easily followed by students.

Purposes of Curriculum

The curriculum serves the following purposes since it is the source of all activities of the institutions:

To provide pupils continuous as well as sequential experiences right from the very beginning of the school onward, that is, through the secondary school on into the college.

To provide effectively for individual differences, ability needs and interests.

To make use of maximum of local skills and resources.

To provide for built in mechanisms, which provide for its continuous and critical re-evaluation.

A good curriculum should draw out cultivate, excite and inspire the full development of the student.

It should create an atmosphere in which students will learn to think critically and constructively, seek the truth and be able to solve problem.

Characteristic of Curriculum

The main characteristics of curriculum are:

It must be mostly based upon the first hand experiences of the pupils from all the significant areas of human being. These experiences are characterized by newness, novelty, challenge, stimulation and creativity. Content receive increasing emphasis as the children move to the higher grades.

It should emphasize intellectual structures; and conceptual themes.

It should provide sufficient scope for aberration, experimentation, independent work, and drawing of inferences and criticism of experimental results obtained in the laboratory. Further it should provide pupils sufficient experiences in formulating problem not only pinpointedly but more and more productively as well. Pupils will thus gain practice in the use of scientific method indirectly at their level of development.

It should provide sufficient scope for the cultivation of scientific skills, interest, attitudes and appreciation.

It should be psychologically sound. It should take into account the theories of learning relevant to biology teaching (Gestalt psychology, Genera School and the work of those psychologists and education's which relates to the Acceleration of Mental Development in particular). Further children's capacities and capabilities, if taken into account, will lead to the development of differentiated curriculum (for meeting individual difference). Incorporating geographical difference in it will be another innovation.

It should aim at bringing about an intelligent and effective adjustment with the environment itself. Further, it should enable pupils to acquire relevant scientific information of subsequent and in the significant areas of human being.

It should foster the growth or development of attitude and skills required for maintaining a planned social order of democratic type. To put more concretely, it should contribute towards democratic living.

It is tested and improved through research, lastly, it should not be narrowly conceived should not be static but dynamic and forward looking, sample adequately both the scientific content and the abilities of the pupils to be developed, should cater to the right use of leisure later on and should be related to the environment in which the children live. Consequently, it will then become exciting, real and imaginative.

Defects in the Curriculum

Though our present day curriculum is jumbling of facts it has been badly criticized but it is difficult to abandon it because of some reasons. In comparison to experience – centred curriculum, the subject –centred curriculum is simple, intelligible and can be easily evaluated. Because of these and some other reasons defective curriculum still persists.

The review of the present curriculum shows that it suffers from the following defects: It is subject-centred and topical. It is academic in nature and deals with the theoretical generalizations. The teacher usually stick to one textbook and deliver lectures on the subject matter without caring much for the interests and activity of the students. It is, therefore, bookish and stereotyped and lays emphasis on the acquisition of knowledge rather than its application on to daily life. It is overcrowded without providing rich and significant contents.

It is examination – ridden. The result is that the teachers as well as the pupils select important portion from the whole syllabus from the examination point of view deleting the unimportant portion, because the worth of the teacher is judged from the pass percentage of the students in the examination and the ability of the student is assessed by the measure of how much he can vomit out in the examination. Thus, the whole process of education becomes a game of hide and seeks between the examiners and the examinee.

It does not cater to the various needs and capacities of the adolescents. In short, we can say that it ignores individual differences. It is a single-track curriculum.

It is cut off from real life outside and is not in accordance with the needs of the pupils and the need of society.

It is rigid and not flexible and also state. The depth of the subject is sacrificed at the expense of vastness of range of topics. It is better to study a few topics thoroughly than to completes so many in a haphazard way.

It outfits the different age groups. The capabilities, interests of different age groups are not taken into account while training the syllabus.

Principles

Curriculum development involves certain principles, which need to be considered to fulfill the requirements of the individuals and the society and to achieve the aims and objectives of the causes and institution. These principles are:

1. **Principles of the nature and objective of the courses**

As every course is started to achieve certain aims and objectives depending on its nature, the curriculum should be in conformity of these goals.

2. **Principle of the duration of the course**

Every course will have its time duration. Depending on the availability of time the curriculum must be constructed.

3. **Principle of the Availability of Resources**

The curriculum implementation requires both manual and material resources. So the curriculum must be practical in nature means considering the availability of teachers, laboratories, equipment, textbooks, evaluations tests, etc.

4. **Principle of the Totality of Experiences**

The curriculum must be facilitator of total experiences needed for a child. Hence in a school child should get total experiences which will help a child in practical life also but not just experiences from a set of subjects.

5. **Principle of Individual Interests**

(a) Principle of utility: The curriculum should meet the daily needs of the children. It should give practical knowledge so as to enjoy the life and to adjust to the changing conditions of life and society.

(b) Principle of vocational requirement: The curriculum should prepare the pupils for future life by providing information about their future vocational requirements, otherwise the schooling will result in a waste.

(c) Principle of creativeness: Every child will have some creativity. The curriculum must provide opportunities to utilize and promote creativeness of the pupils.

(d) Principle of development of innate powers: The innate powers of the children must be drawn out and sharpened by the curriculum. The pupils can be kept in place of a scientist so as to develop their innate powers.

(e) Principle of child centredness: This principle says that curriculum should be according to the needs of the pupils at the particular age.

(f) Principle of Elasticity and Variety: It should not be rigid but should be changed to suit the changing needs of the pupils and the society. It should be flexible and broad based.

(g) Principle of Leisure Time Pursuits: The curriculum should provide work for the leisure time of the children.

(h) Principle of Activity Centredness: There should be emphasis on learning by doing. More provision should be made for individual laboratory work and other field experiences.

(i) Principle of Forward Looking: It should help the child in adjustment and prepare him for full and effective adult life.

(j) Principle of Moral Values: To live in the society, as a successful citizen the curriculum should develop

the social norms and mores. Working, resources such as teachers, laboratories, equipments, library facilities, etc.

Example If classification of plants and animals is going on in theory periods then at the same time we should have all the specimens in the laboratory also so that classification topic can be taught in comprehensive manner, i.e., including theory and practical work.

4. **Principle of totality of experiences**

According to this principle Biology curriculum should provide various learning experiences that will inculcate various skills such as taking – sections, dissections, observation, drawing skills, manipulating the apparatus, collection of data, field trips for particular purpose (collection of species) at particular season.

5. **Principle of Individual Interests**

According to this principle individual needs and interests must be taken care of and considered while developing curriculum.

6. **Principle of the Society Interests**

(a) Principle of vocational Requirements: curriculum should have provisions to meet the vocational requirements of the complex organization of the society.

(b) Principle of Integrity of the Society: Curriculum should develop integrative attitude in the minds of pupils.

(c) Principle of conservation: The curriculum should help in preserving and transmitting the traditions, standards of conduct on which the culture and civilization depend.

(d) Principle of International Consciousness: The knowledge about the contributions of scientists to make, the interdependence of nations etc. can help the children in developing international consciousness.

Explanation

1. **Principle of the Nature and objective of the course:**

According to this principle curriculum should be designed in such a manner that it should achieve the objectives according to the nature of the subject.

Example: Life-sciences is dynamic in nature, for information goes on adding up according to the new inventions so curriculum should be designed accordingly such as activity based and experiment based.

2. **Principle of the Duration of the Course**

Biology curriculum is having different activities such as field-trips, practical work, excursions, exhibitions which are equally important, so each activity should be given appropriate time.

3. **Principle of Availability of resources**

For an efficient curriculum, it should take care of all the resources for its effective working. Resources such as teachers, laboratories, equipments, library facilities etc.

Example: If classification of plants and animals is going on in theory periods then at the same time we should have all the specimens in the laboratory also so that classification topic can be taught in comprehensive manner, i.e., including theory and practical work.

4. **Principle of totality of Experiences**

According to this principle Biology curriculum should provide various learning experiences that will inculcate various skills such as taking - sections, Dissections, observations Drawing skills, Manipulating the apparatus, collection of data, field trips for particular purpose (collection of species) at particular season.

5. **Principle of Individual Interests**

According to this principle individual needs and interests must be taken care of and considered while developing curriculum age interest, needs, must be taken care of in the educative process. Slogan "know the child is very important because there is diversity in interest, attitude, aptitude of the child. Individual differences are bound to be there. Some are gifted; some are average, while some are below average. Therefore we need flexible curriculum. We have the same curriculum for all, which is not good thing. Curriculum should be in continuity, should be goal oriented, according to the constitution of the country related to the needs of the society and should lead to all-round development of the child.

6. **Principle of the Society Interests**

A child is a social being and his capacities, interests and needs find development in the society and for the society. He is to be prepared for social life and therefore the present social life should be related in the curriculum. The social adjustment is also necessary and therefore the curriculum must be according to the local needs of the society. Depending on the development in that particular area like agriculture, industry, fishing etc.

Approaches to Curriculum Organization

The curriculum can be organized depending on the objectives to be achieved. Majority five approaches such as integrated or Disciplinary, Flexible or Structured, Conceptual or Factual, Process or Content and Teacher-centred or pupil-centered. Any one or Combinations of these approaches can be used in developing the curriculum.

Disciplinary Approach

Biology is such a subject that it has its own concepts, facts, theories, explanation etc., which make it as a sole subject. And though it is a branch of science, it becomes a major subject. Thus, it is taught by the Disciplinary Approach.

Systems of Organizing Curriculum

The content organizations in the curriculum needs are to be considered carefully depending on the objectives to be achieved and facilities that are available. The content can be organized in different ways.

1. Logical order Method

In logical order method the topics or lessons will be arranged in an orderly manner from simple to complex stages, from abstract to concrete knowledge. So that student can easily understand the lessons and is able to relate the knowledge gained from previous lesson to following lesson. This method will give comprehensive and integrated knowledge about the subject. This arrangement of lesson will be in the same class or it can be spread to some other classes of the course.

2. Concentric Method

The topics, in this method, will find a place in different classes of different years of a course in a progressive manner. The content will be included from simple to complex as the classes progress so as to make the pupils understand the content according to capabilities that present in chronological and mental ages.

3. Topic Method

In this method, the content selected will be explained in detail in the same class at the same point. Once completed, there will be no future learning about that topic. This method can be used in covering the basic concepts in the curriculum. Because certain topics or content is important to be taught at the particular age, like the basic concepts, this cannot be extended to further classes.

4. Psychological Method

The subject matter in this method will be selected based on the psychological level of the pupils. Depending on the mental ages, the content will be chosen. Mental age is the major factor in the placement of subject materials. For example, early investigations have shown that the efficient work in beginning reading requires a mental age of six and one-half years. Later investigations have shown that the mental age required for successful progress in reading depends largely upon the simplicity of materials and upon how reading is taught. Chronological age is important in curriculum to understand certain complex process and to learn various skills. This method emphasizes that curriculum should be based on psychological level of the pupils such as interests, intelligence, abilities, past experiences, motivation, etc.

5. Historical Method

Arrangement of subject matter takes place as per its historical development. The content will be linked with contemporary issues, inventions etc. With this method students will be able to remember development of certain concept, theory etc. for e.g. how cell theory was proposed, how the invention of different scientist contributed it and is it recently applicable or it has been modified.

6. Seasonal Arrangement of Lessons Method

The lesson will be arranged in the curriculum according to availability of natural resources. It will be absurd to teach about rain in summer or about a frog's life history in non-seasons. Hence the arrangement or content follows the seasons.

(1) Logical method

(Example)

(i) CELL:

(i) (Cell theory, cell shape, size number of cells – unicellular and multicellular organisms)

(ii) Types of cells? ? Plant cell
? Animal cell

(iii) Cell structure:- cell organelles -

(Cytoplasm, Plasmamembrane, Endoplasmic reticulum, Ribosome's, Golgibody, Lysosome, Mitochondrion, Chloroplast, Centrasome, cilium and flagellum, Nucleus, cell wall, vacuoles Intracellular substance)

(iv) Cell Division:-

Mitosis, Meiosis

(2) Concentric method:

For example: Environmental Pollution

CHART

Psychological method:

(i) Awareness about Population Explosion
(ii) Reasons of Population Explosion
(iii) Effects of Population Explosion on Natural resources—Economical aspects and social aspects
(iv) Necessities for population control
(v) Method of Population control.

Topic Method:

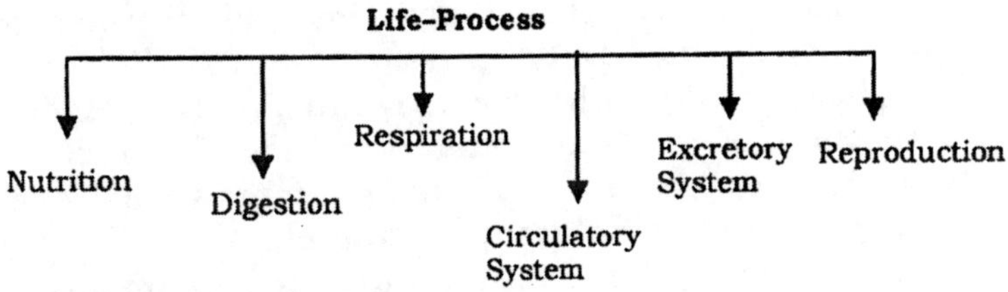

History Method: Example DNA

- Discovery of Nucleus
- Role of Nucleus in heredity
- Identification of chromosomes and genes
- 3 – dimensional structure of DNA by Wilkinson
- Double helical structure of DNA by Watson and Crick.

Seasonal Arrangement of Lesson Method

For Example classification of Plants.

Algae, Fungi belonging to the division Thallophyta and Bryophyta (Moss, Riccia) are easily available in rainy season so theory classes for this topic should be arranged accordingly.

Styles of Curriculum Development

Basically three styles of curriculum can be identified.

(a) Instrumental
(b) Interactive
(c) Individualistic

Instrumental type of curriculum developed in the post-Sputnik era in late 1950's to satisfy the need of the society, and to prepare students having instrumental knowledge. It means students after schooling when come in society, community or work field they should have working knowledge in the demanding situations. Meaning thereby they should have practical knowledge of solving the problem and doing the action, but not just theoretical knowledge.

The interactive type of curriculum in the mid-sixties followed instrumental type of curriculum. Because during this period a curriculum reform was extended to other aspects of the school programme and other sections of the school community.

Other aspects, which came into picture of school curriculum, were co-curricular activities. This includes, debate, elocution, quiz programmes, different competitions such as essay writing etc.

It also includes different cultural programmes of the school one of them is Annual function. All this aspects were included to develop thinking, logical reasoning, open mindedness, rationale explanation in a student to make him interactive and active member in the society with a balanced personality.

At the end of 1960's Individualistic style have been evolved. By this period another set of assumptions came into focus, which laid emphasis on individual differences. In a school, in class there are lot many individual differences among students, may be at physical level, emotional level, cognition level. The difference may lie at socio-economic status. So this style of curriculum will cater to the needs of all type of students thus having individualistic approach and focus is on the development of the individual.

Each of these styles was different in terms of goals, domains, and teaching technique and evolution technique. It will be clearer by the chart given back. Each style has its strengths and weaknesses.

Styles of Curriculum Development

Styles	*Instrumental*	*Interactive*	*Individualistic*
Major Goals	Utilitarian, Job career oriented	Society oriented, Social development	Personal or individual development
Implicit Values	People as things (competition)	People as social animals (Interaction and co-operation)	People as individuals (idiosyncratic /self development).
Subject Domains	Disciplinary	Interdisciplinary (humanities, General Sciences, social studies) Affective	Gross interdisciplinary (Science and humanities mix) creative
Taxonomic	Cognitive	Affective	Creative
Domains Materials	Highly structured (Teachers hand books, students workbooks, prescribed texts etc.)	Loosely structured (student's packages, teacher's guides, multimedia etc.)	Unstructured (modular based, resource banks retrieval system).
Teacher's Role	As Director	As Manager	As Assistant
Teaching Techniques	Lecture, Discovery, Inductive Inquiry	Group projects, Problem solving, Discussions	Self-instructional techniques, practical tasks.
Evaluation Techniques	Teacher evaluation-mainly objective (pre-specified goals)	Teacher evaluation mainly subjective	Self-evaluation (goals identified during the process of learning).

Modern Trends in Biology Curriculum

(1) Biological Sciences Curriculum Study (B.S.C.S.)

(a) (BSCS) – High School Biology:

The BSCS was established for the improvement of biological education at all levels. The school structures in the United States are 6-3-3 (elementary-junior high – senior high school), 8-4 (elementary – secondary), 6-

2-4, 7-2-3 (elementary – middle-secondary) and other local variations. At the elementary stage different disciplines are integrated and at tenth, eleventh and twelfth levels, students study only one science. Significant numbers of students study Biology in the last grade (age group 15-16). Two biology courses have been developed by BSCS. One that is offered when the students enter 10th grade, the other one is offered either in 11th or 12th grade after successful passing the first course. Both the courses are of one-year duration. Students can offer other disciplines (Physics or Chemistry) also depending upon their interest.

The BSCS has developed three parallel courses for average and above – average students. A separate course was developed for retarded students. It was thought that no one approach to modern biology is necessarily more valid or better for the high school students than any other approach. There have been no data available to indicate that one approach or one kind of Biology (e.g.) ecological, biochemical or evolutionary) is more satisfactory or valid in presenting the subject to the secondary school students. Thus, three alternative approaches, the *blue (molecular approach),*

Green (ecological approach and yellow (evolutionary approach) versions of BSCS High school Biology were prepared in 1960 on an experimental basis.

The three versions were built around the *nine basic themes* in Biology

(i) Change of living things through time: Evolution
(ii) Diversity of type and unity of pattern in living things.
(iii) The genetic continuity of life.
(iv) The complementarities of organism and environment.
(v) The biological roots of behaviour.
(vi) The complementarities of structure and function.
(vii) Regulation and homeostasis: Preservation of life in the face of change.
(viii) Science as inquiry
(ix) The history of biological conceptions.

All the textbooks represent a balanced one-year course. The titles of the books are:

(i) Biological Science: Molecules to Man (Blue Version)

(ii) High School Biology (Green Version)

(iii) Biological Science: An inquiry into life (Yellow Version).

Other instructional materials besides textbooks are as follows:

(i) Teacher's guide

(ii) Biology teacher's hand book

(iii) Laboratory block

(iv) Single topic films

(v) Biological technique films.

(vi) A book for retarded students entitled as 'Patterns and Processes of Science'.

The principle objective of the BSCS programme of sixties was to re-establish close contacts of high school Biology with current conceptual and methodological developments in Biological Sciences while maintaining psychological and pedagogical ideas about the teaching - learning process as they apply to 10th grade student. Except green version, the blue and yellow versions are psychologically and pedagogically unsound for majority of the tenth grades.

(b) BSCS Senior Secondary Biology Programme

After publishing books for 10th grade, the BSCS prepared text for teaching at the 11th or 12th grade. Only one-year course was developed which can be taught either in 11th or 12th grade. The BSCS Biology second course entitled, 'The Interaction of Experiments and Ideas' was developed to increase the understanding of concepts taught in earlier one year course (10th grade). This course is more laboratory oriented than the earlier (tenth grade) and a students spends most of his time working on laboratory experiments which are increasingly open-ended. That is, they present problem situations, which a student himself must learn, how to solve and for some of the problems, no satisfactory solution has yet been reached by the scientists in the laboratory.

The *limitations* of BSCS biology programmes are as follows.

(i) No biology programmes have been developed for lower grades.

(ii) The broad BSCS objective of Biology Education possibly cannot be dully achieved by these two courses. The objectives are to educate students to, think logically, solve problems, develop and investigate ideas, and bring an inquiry attitude to new situations.

The Nuffield Biology Project

The project was started in December 1961 to prepare new science curricula for the primary and secondary school of Britain. In American high schools, three science subjects are taught separately in successive years, at least in the later grades. But in British Schools, two or even three sciences (Physics, Chemistry and Biology) are studied side by side. This system has necessitated careful synchronization of certain sections of the three Nuffield courses, i.e., Physics, Chemistry and Biology.

This project has considered the requirements of children within the age group 11-16 who will take General Certificate of Education (GCE) at ordinary level. The main aim of the programme is to develop scientific outlook among students. This aim is to be achieved through texts and guides, which are based on experimental approach. The instructional materials are briefly described below.

(i) Textbooks

Textbooks follow the critical approach to the facts obtained by biologists. Instead of accepting facts blindly, some experimental data have been provided to give students an opportunity to interpret and to draw their own conclusion.

The course is divided into five sections each lasting for a year. The first two years (age group 11-13) represent the introductory phase, while the remaining three (age group 13-16) constitute intermediate phase.

The aim of the introductory course is to provide training in observation, recording, and formulation of hypothesis and making simple deductions. In the early stages, the work is largely descriptive, but it becomes more quantitative towards the end of the second year. From the third year onward the approach is more rigorous and quantitative and the design of experiments is open-ended type.

(ii) **Teacher's guide**

This helps a teacher to teach topics effectively. Suggestions for practical work are included in these, e.g., construction of apparatus, preparation of reagents etc.

(iii) **Film-loops**

Each film-loop is of three minutes duration. These deal with the processes, which cannot be easily performed in the school laboratory. These are projected with 800.E projector.

Biology Projects: India

NCERT is contributing a lot for the development of biology / life sciences programmes.

(i) Programme for 11-year schooling

NCERT undertook a major programme to prepare model textbooks in different subjects for schools. For this purpose, the council formed the central committee for Educational Literature to guide and direct the programme. Panels of specialists were set up by the Central Committee to develop curricula and to write books, teacher's resource books and other materials on school subjects. The Biology Text -Book Panel under the Chairmanship of Prof. P. Maheswari, the then Head of the Department of Botany, Delhi University, was establishment in 1963. This panel developed biology textbooks for higher secondary classes (9-11). The textbooks were developed to incorporate contemporary and fundamental knowledge of Biology.

The course has been divided into seven sections. The first section deals, with a few basics about Biology. After this brief introduction, the student is informed about diversity in plants in second and third sections. The fourth section describes important physiological processes in plant and animals, in a very simple and interesting way. The fifth section highlights the comparative account of the different modes of reproduction in plants and animals. The sixth section conveys fundamental knowledge about heredity, evolutionary process and ecological systems. The last section emphasizes biosocial problems, for instance, human diseases, interdependence of plants and animals, the role of biology in human welfare, etc.

(ii) **Programmes for +2 system**

NCERT constituted a Biology Editorial Board for classes XI –XII under the chairmanship of M.R.N. Prasad, Department of Zoology, Delhi University to develop biology programme for +1 and +2 under 12-year schooling pattern. The aim of developing these books is to incorporate social problems concerning social justice, rural development and building a secular, socialist and democratic republic. The textbook entitled 'Biology – A Text Book for Higher Secondary Classes': Part –I and Part –II (Vol. I. and Vol. II) was developed in 1977-78.

This book follows disciplinary and conceptual approach. There is a scope for adaptability. The book is organized into units. Part-I deals with anatomy and physiology of plants animals, morphology and taxonomy of plants and finally bio-social problems. Part II (Vol. I. and II) highlights cell biology, genetics, developmental biology and applications of Biology to human welfare.

Marking scheme of H.S.C.E board
Practical examination

1. Bio chemical test (any one to be given) (1) Egg albumin – protein (2) Any oil. (3) Starch carbohydrate.	Marks 5	*Chapter in the practical Book.* 1
2. Section cutting, staining, Mounting and Viva Voce (Any one)	09	

Item	Marks	
(1) T.S of Maize root		2
(2) T.S of Sunflower stem		3
(3) T.S of Maize stem		3
(4) T.S of Maize leaf		4
(5) T.S of Sunflower leaf		4
3. Charts of frog systems (Any two charts) from each chart any one part can be indicated for identification all questions to be answered orally (viva voce)	05	
(1) Digestive system.		5,10
(2) Arterial system.		6,10
(3) Anterior Venous system.		7,10
(4) Posterior Venous system.		7,10
(5) Urinogential system of male and female frog		8,10
(6) Nervous system.		9,10
4. Identify and describe according to the instructions: -		
SP1 – Structure of flower, seed and seed germination.		11,12
SP2 – Adaptations of plants: - Root stem and leaf.		13,14
SP3 – Adaptations of plants: - Root, stem and leaf.		13,14
SP4 – Adaptations of plants: - Root, stem and leaf.		13,14
SP5 – Plant tissues: Meristem or any other tissue.		15
SP6 – Bone of frog: - Axial skeleton.		16
SP7 – Bone of frog: - Appendicle skeleton.		17
SP8 – Frog: organ Histology-permanent slides.		18
SP9 – Frog: organ Histology-permanent slides.		18
SP10 – Frog: Animal tissues.		19, 20, 21
SP11 – Frog: Metamorphosis and embryo development.		22
SP12 – Human chromosomes, chromosomal defects and sex determination in man.		23
SP13 – Chromatography or plant physiology experiments.		24, 25, 26 and 27
5 Journal	05	
Total –	50	

SP = specimen

10
Teaching Aids

Teaching Aids enhances teaching and makes the teaching learning process efficient and effective. It is able to arouse interest of the student. It should be related to the teaching and the levels of students. It should not replace the teacher but should aid in teaching. Teaching aid facilitates teaching.

Importance of Teaching Aids

1. *Facilitates teaching – learning process* by helping in teaching of abstract concept. The verbal input can be related to the teaching aid input and thus verbalism is reduced. Verbalism creates different impression on child's mind. Explanation becomes easily, i.e., abstract becomes more concrete. It will save time and energy e.g. concept is brought closer. For example if orchid is taught it grows in NEFA region but teacher brings a model in class and the students get the idea of the concept.
2. *Helps in concentration*: The teaching aid appeals to more than 1 sense and thus, it leads to concentration. The picture is magnified so that the students are able to remember for a longer time.
3. *Makes teaching interesting*: As the atmosphere is different from the routine one the students find it more interesting.
4. *Interaction*: While teaching it increases the interactions in the classroom by the retention power. Thus, interaction and retention are combined.

5. Its, economical as compared to excursion or a field visit. If a teacher is teaching about marine ecosystem best would be to take them to a site. But taking students out would cost much more than showing a documentary or video. So we can say it is economical.

6. Helps in developing skills like observation, psychomotor, experimenting, drawing, i.e., once the students see the teaching aid they can improvise it.

7. Abstract ideas which are processing in mind can be shown as visual without using words, e.g., cartoon strips.

8. Teaching aid is an eye catcher because when we use different type of natural colour schemes it catches your eyes and helps in better teaching – learning.

9. It reduces the barrier of time and place.

10. Finally, it saves the energy of the teacher.

11. Helps in problem solving, i.e., when performing demonstration then leaving it for the students to think and thus helps in problem solving.

12. To inculcate scientific attitude gives training in scientific method.

13. Pupils get chance to touch, feel handle and manipulate things.

14. Students are motivated to do work and they work of their own accord and not out of the fear of the teacher.

Principles of Using Teaching Aid

1. *Content relevance:* The teaching aid should be relevant to the content. The content relevance can be found through content analysis. Which can be done before school begins and prepare the teaching aid. Teacher has to prepare a list of teaching aids to be used.

2. Teaching aid should be based on the **objectives** that have to be achieved, i.e., whether it's knowledge, understanding psychomotor.

3. *Appropriate time of showing*: - How do we decide that its appropriate use of time? It is done at different stages at which it could be used. Teaching aid can be used either at the beginning, middle or at the end, i.e., during introduction, explanation or evaluation stage.

4. If more than one teaching aid is used it must clarify the concept and not to create confusion. It should link various concepts one after other.

5. *Participation of students*: - While using teaching aid a teacher should not be engrossed in the teaching aid but should also see that the students are also participating in the teaching learning process.

6. *Principle of visibility and Display*: - Teaching aid should be visible to the entire class and should always try to clarify the concept and not making it more complex.

7. *Principle of Evaluation*: - The knowledge taught why, what and how of teaching aid has to be evaluated. What is shown? How is it represented? Inter-relationship among the subcomponents etc.

Classification of teaching aids

1. Audio. 2. Visual.
3. Audio Visual.

UNESCO classified it as follows: -

1. Flat material – Black board, Glass board charts.
2. Audio material – Cassette.
3. Three dimensional – Models.
4. Film and related equipment – Motion pictures.
5. Still projections – OHP slides.
6. Folk media and theatre – Role play, drama.
7. T.V. Video.
8. Computer.

Cobon (1968) found 1% of what is learnt is from sense of taste.

1.5% of what is learnt is from sense of taste.

3.5% of what is learnt is from sense of smell.

11% of what is learnt is from sense of hearing.

83% of what is learnt is from sense of sight.

Retention of students is dependent on the following factors.

10% of what they read.

20% of what they hear.

30% of what they see.

50% of what they hear/see.

70% of what they say.

90% of what they say they are doing.

1. **Flat materials**: Charts, blackboard, white boards, flash cards, flannel board, Roll up board, magnet board, bulletin board, graphs, photographs, maps, cartoons are e.g.'s of flat material.

a. **Charts:** They are two dimensional type.

(i) Diagrammatic charts: - Here symbols are used which are geometrical in shape.

(ii) Tree chart: - Naturally dividing content into various branches of a tree. E.g. evolutionary trends.

(iii) Pictorial charts: - Pictures are stuck up on chart paper example's Mendel's experiment.

(iv) Multiple leaf chart: - The concept is unfolded part by part leaf after leaf, e.g., parts of flowers.

(v) Flow chart: It indicates the flow of content.

(a) **Black board**: It is the most popular.

(b) **White boards**: They are also called magnetic board. Used mainly where respiratory trouble is there. Different special coloured pens are used.

(c) **Flash Cards**: They are A4 size used in primary class. It is two dimensional where pictures can be drawn to teach a concept.

(d) **Flannel board**: Used to display different details for teaching a topic. It can also be in form of bulletin board. Some puzzles, G.K. questions can also be displayed.

2. **3 – D Materials**: The models can be of two types, viz. static model and working model.

(a) **Static Model**: - e.g. DNA and RNA, eye, heart, ear that are imitation of reality.

(b) **Working model**: - Transmission of nerve impulse circulation of blood. The model should have appropriate magnification so that it doesn't have illusive and unreal effect.

(c) **Mock ups**: - When the direct first hand experience is either impractical or impossible. Mockups can be used. A mock up may be defined as an operating mode, designed to be worked with directly by the learner for specific training or analysis. Mock up is an imitation of a real thing. Mock ups are very useful in giving training in complex skills. For example while giving training for interview, we first give a few mockup sessions. To well verse the candidate with various skills required.

(d) **Dioramas**: - A diorama is a three dimensional scene in depth incorporating a group of modeled objects and figures in a natural setting. Dioramas are very effective in the teaching of social and Biological sciences. For example in museum when a stuffed lion is set in its natural setting in a large glass box. It is a diorama or even a glass box depicting dinosaurs in their natural setting.

3. **Audio Material**: These aids involve the use of sense of hearing.

(a) Radio, (b) Gramophone. (c) Tape Recorder.

(a) **Radio**:- It is an instructional aid which is now coming into limelight. Programme for school children is now a regular feature of A.I.R. and B.B.C.

- Radio gives current news of the whole world, we can also hear talks of great scientists in different parts of the world.
- It brings sense of participation on the part of pupils.
- It adds variety to the classroom technique and removes monotony. The pupils feel interested when they hear something pleasant and valuable.
- It is a means of supplementing, vitalizing correlating and modernizing the materials of textbook.

(b) **Tape Recorders**: This aid can be used by teacher especially for introducing a lesson. Talks by eminent persons can be recorded and reproduced in class for a number of times. It can be used to record songs of birds and distinctive background noises.

4. **Still Projections**: - Still projections are the visual projections. They can be of four types.

(a) **Slide Projector**: - The slides are projected by an instrument equipped with a powerful light source in a lamp house and carrier for holding slides of suitable sizes. It is a simple mechanism and usually a double slide carrier is fitted into the projector so that when one slide is being projected on the screen a second slide can be kept ready. These projectors can be operated and focused by remote controls. It is also possible to record the narration in a tape recorder and latter may be booked up to the projector in such a way to give necessary commentary without the help of teacher.

(b) **Over head projector OHP**: -

The name comes from the fact that the projected image is behind and over the head of the speaker. In over head projection a transparent visual is placed on a horizontal stage on top of a light source. The light passes through this transparency and then is reflected at an angle on to the screen at the back of the speaker.

Whenever one prepares a transparency following criteria should be kept in mind.

1. As far as possible write in capital.
2. Write only important points.
3. Too much data should not be taken on a single sheet.
4. Colours should be properly used to highlight.

(c) **Epidiascope**

Epidiascope is a combination of episcope and Dias cope. It is used to enlarge book diagrams for preparation of charts by the teacher. It is not advisable to resort to epidiascope projection for normal classroom teaching.

1. The machine is very large and heavy.
2. It requires a dark room to use it.

5. **Motion Pictures**: - Motion picture as an aid to teaching is inferior to direct experience. But in some cases motion picture will be able to provide the expected learning outcome better than even direct experience. The bright image on the screen with the associated sound is more realistic if it is in colour. It provides a vivid, dynamic visual and is remembered longer than any visual presentation.

Motion picture films can be classified as entertainment films and educational films include films about technology, travel films, sports, health, informational about industry, flora and fauna, historical etc.

(a) **Films**: No scientific invention can claim to have rendered more service to education than the cinematograph, but the schools in India cannot make use of this privilege because of financial difficulties. The films make the concept clear, durable and realistic.

The importance of films is seen particularly when educational films are shown to the children.

(i) Classroom films.
(ii) Industrial films.
(iii) School made films.
(iv) Documentary films.
(v) News – reels.

(i) **Classroom films**: These films are directly concerned with classroom teaching and can be divided into:

(a) **Process films**: - These films explain the different stages involved in the process, e.g., formation of rain, change of season etc.

(b) **Films for general information**: - These films are not directly concerned with the curriculum but which form a basis for an integrated and correlated study.

(c) **For demonstration of a skill**: - Certain films, which show demonstration of a particular experiment beyond the scope of school department.

(d) **Revision films**: - There are some films in which a wide range of material is assembled in one short film.

(e) **Films dramatizing an event or episode**: - Films can also be used in depicting the life histories of scientists, history of some discovery or invention.

(f) **Industrial films**: - These films show the mechanics of different types of machines i.e. the different parts of a machine and the function of each part.

(g) **School made films**: - They encourage the students. These films are prepared by the school showing different activities of science clubs or science fairs.

(h) **Documentary films**: - These films cover a wide variety of subjects. These films are an industrial on social themes. These films provide a background to scientific studies.

(i) **Newsreels**: - These are also produced by the Government of India and deal with the current events.

Methods of Using a Film:

Methods of using a film is important than the film itself the teacher should make all necessary arrangements for projector, room, operator etc. He should notify the day, data and time of showing the film. A thorough background of the subject matter covered in the film should be given to the students before hand in order to secure greatest benefit. After the film is shown, there should be questioning, comments and discussions to clear up the difficulties.

6. **Television**: - The T.V. combines both elements of radio and the potentialities of the film.

Keeping in view the scarcity of qualified personnel and lack of well equipped laboratories. The television is made use of in teaching in classroom syllabus. This type of programme is called instructional television. In such programmes the teacher designated as the T.V. teacher performs the experiment or delivers the lecture before T.V. camera in the studio and this is received on the T.V. sets fitted in each classroom out of 40 minutes period the first five minutes are reserved for testing previous knowledge of students by the class teacher in order to prepare them of the lesson. Next twenty minutes are for T.V. lesson and remaining fifteen minutes for follow up work.

7. **Video Programmes**: - These programmes can be developed by the teacher.

Procedure for developing video programme

(i) Select a content for which you have to develop a video programme.

(ii) Then write a script of the content, which should be frame to frame. It is also called as screenplay. In each frame what will be shown plus the background and dialogue must be written. Here some content enrichment should be done according to the age interest and ability of the student.

(iii) Once the script is ready send it to experts. One expert from media, another from subject (for which the film is made), third should be pedagogical expert and last should be the language expert. After the comments of the experts modify the content. The teacher can decide which changes are essential. After due modification. You can now do the shooting. For shooting following points must be kept in mind.

(i) There should not be any kind of monotony. i.e., variety should be there.

(ii) Background should be different in colour. i.e., the presenter's colours and background colour should be opposite.

(iii) Shooting should be done from different angles. Variety of stimulus should be there.

(iv) The people involved should be energetic and not dull otherwise programme will be bore.

(v) You can involve some guest for a low budget video.

(vi) Once the shooting is over, editing is necessary. Where the technician and shooter sit and edits the programme. This is done because the program is shot at different angles. It may not be in sequence and so for making the program successful sequencing of programme is important therefore editing is done.

(vii) In school it is easy to shoot as location and properties are available and also people are available.

8. **Computer**: There are some packages which are readymade and available that can be shown to students. Computer if attached to LCD projector can also act as a still projection. Internet is another useful resource that a teacher can use to enrich the material and even project it in the classroom.

(a) One should know the basics of computers.

(b) One can develop frames along with graphics, i.e., linear or branched.

(c) Write the matter in branched/linear form and then write a programme.

Once the programme is ready send it to experts education, technical, language. They will give suggestions incorporate those suggestions.

(d) After modification prepare computer program.

(e) Then show the programme to students who will give their difficulties.

(f) Also give test by which teacher can find out the students difficulty, which the students don't say. This can be seen by their test score.

(g) After finding difficulty you can improve your programme.

There can be discussion with other teachers for suggestions. The student's can use the programme for their self-study also.

9. **Folk theatre, Drama, play**: There are number of street plays which give messages on biological points and environmental problems like population, pollution, vaccination, health and hygiene, small family norms, Biogas etc. such plays can be played in community and classrooms.

(ii) **Folk shows** depict the socio-cultural relations and values of a country rather than the language.

(iii) **Theatre**: is also important for language. They are good and are based on some illustrative novels, stories that can be enacted, to give the feel of a particular time period.

10. **Aids through Activity**:

1. **Field Trips and Excursions**

Excursions and visits to places of scientific interest provide opportunities for direct experience and thus the learning becomes more interesting.

When excursions are undertaken by students of an educational institution the main aim is not only recreation and pleasure but also gaining additional knowledge through direct experience. Hence, it is necessary to select a suitable place to visit.

When excursions are undertaken for the specific purpose of development of knowledge of pupils it becomes a study tour or styled as 'field trip'. During the field trip the pupil has concrete learning experiences in a real situation, which has been undertaken with a specific purpose.

Types of field trips:

(a) **Local school trips**: - These are arranged to various parts and sections of one's own school building and grounds to see procedure, equipment and materials, e.g., measuring distances, studying trees, flowers etc.

(b) **Community trips**: It is a usual trip to some nearby place like a zoo or a museum. It takes longer than the regular class period of the school must cooperate and contribute something valuable. Teachers must guide and lead the pupils in the preparation of possible exhibits. The explanations for the exhibits must as far as possible.

Arrangement of exhibits and planning of the exhibits should be done so they may serve their purpose.

Museums

Museums are a wonderful medium for public education. They are institutions that collect and preserve original objects and specimens and use them for research and for educational displays. Every school can build its own museum with the help of teachers and students. Museums are not only places of visit by pupils but in many countries serve as sources of instructural materials to schools.

Demonstrations

Demonstration is a technique, which is often used by all teachers teaching various subjects. Ideas, skills, attitudes and processes can be demonstrated.

The teacher must give chance to the students to perform demonstrations in the classroom.

All aids must be arranged in order to avoid.

(c) **Tours**: - They may last for several days. Proper planning and organization for execution are essential.

(d) **Inter school visits**:- (i) A specialized group or science club visits the corresponding organization of the other school for exchange of ideas to mutual interest.

(ii) A group or a class or even all sections of that class visit another school for half a day or a day.

(f) **Individual trips**: - Here a pupil or a group of pupils may take this because of an assignment or some responsibility in connection will some curricular or specialized interest.

Thus the field trips or excursion requires planning, preparation, execution, follow up and evaluation.

Exhibitions

Exhibitions are familiar items in our environment. The exhibitions that are arranged in schools are usually planned to communicate something valuable to parents, public and students.

Exhibition is one of the effective modes of mass communication and instruction on a large scale.

Self-activity is fostered on the part of those who take part in the exhibition. Individual talent, fantacies and skills are exhibited. Team spirit is encouraged, as conduct of an exhibition is a co-operative effort.

Exhibitions must be an annual affair. All sections confusion, experiments must be effective. Demonstrations, which are simple, should be chosen, large size apparatus should be used, control experiments should be provided to clarify details, and demonstration should be done with some purpose.

Thus, the aids used in Teaching or in the process of Instruction always brings about effective teaching. These aids are intended to impart knowledge to the pupils through senses to ensure quick and effective learning. The learning through sense is more permanent than mechanical learning. It is admitted that we learn through the senses and the senses of sight and hearing have a greater share in the process. Man depended upon the sight long before he felt the need of speech. But it should always be borne in mind that these aids should be used as aids to teaching and should not replace the teacher but revolutionize other methods of teaching.

Some difficulties and suggestions in the use of Audio - visual Aids

(a) Financial problem:

Ours is a poor country and it will be over ambitious for us to demand the costly apparatus like Projectors, Computers, Television etc from the Government.

(b) Absence of good film libraries, museums of Audio-visual education in the Regional and Central Audio. Visual education centres.

(c) Absence of electricity is a hurdle in the effective use of the Audio-Visual aids.

(d) Improper selection of films. The films selected by the teachers are not in co-ordination with classroom teaching nor the teachers care to integrate them.

(e) Lack of facilities for training teachers. Teachers trained in the use of the Audio-Visual aids are not available nor is there any provision for training them.

(f) Films are not prepared according to the need and conditions of our country.

(g) Indifferences of teachers. Due to the improper planning, lethargy of teachers and absence of proper preparation, correct presentation, appropriate application and discussion and essential follow up work, the aids have not proved their full usefulness.

11
Learning Biology Through Activities

There are many activities that can make biology teaching live and interesting. Let us study about them one by one.

What are Field Trips?

- Are purposeful visits to places of scientific interests and provide valuable experience in the process of science learning.
- Provide students a first hand knowledge of science and stimulate their interests and motivate them to learn.
- Field trip term can be applied to any activity outside the classroom in which the pupils participate.
- A field trip may vary in duration and organization from one to a few hours to an extensively organized lasting a day or more.
- For full benefit, a field trip must be carefully and properly planned.
- It should be considered as a holiday trip though it is a sort of enjoyment but be considered as a serious undertaking.

Purpose of Field Trips

- For collecting various types of seeds leaves, fruits, flowers, rocks etc.

- Studying the habits of migratory birds.
- Learning about the habit and habitat of animals in natural habitat like forests and artificial habitats like Zoos, Sanctuaries etc.
- Studying animal behaviour,
- Learning about cultural practices like Fish Culture, Prawn, Pearl, Lobster etc.
- Knowing how silk is processed from silk worms in Factories.
- Honey and lac production.
- Visit to Family Planning centres and Population control centres.
- Visit to Veterinary Centres to learn about how animal care is provided.
- Dairy visit to get information about how milk is processed and learn about cryopreservations.
- Understanding hybridization through visits to Genetic Engineering Centres.
- Learning about wild species and cultivated species through visits to forests and farms respectively.
- Visits to pharma Industries to understand role of biotechnology in field of medicine.
- Trips to science exhibitions, symposium, seminars.

How to Make Field Trips a Rich Educational Experience

Planning

- The visit or excursion should be planned well in advance with the active co-operation of teacher and pupils in the light of its purpose.
- Includes the formation of the purpose of visit, management with the school time table and regular school work, obtaining of permission of the owner or person in charge of the place to be visited, routed to be traveled, the time schedule, arrangement of the transport and lodging facilities, the expenditure to be borne by the

pupils, the luggage and other necessary articles to be taken along etc.

- The most important aspect of planning is to arrange for finance.

Finance Arrangement

- After listing out the probable field trips during an academic year, it is very essential to make a rough estimate about the total expenditure.
- After accounting for the total expenditure, it is estimated as to how much expenditure should be borne by the school as well as by the Individuals.
- Prior Sanction of the Accounts Department is to be sought.
- It is also to be seen whether any concession is possible for the student's in railway, bus fares etc.
- The expenditure should be in terms of the financial status of school and aids reserved for such trips.
- Teacher Incharge should submit a detailed list of the number of students, place of visit, the duration of stay, the mode of travel, lodging facilities, the necessary articles to be taken along etc.
- Teacher should be resourceful enough to collect grants for the trips.
- The fee structure should be such that a part of it is to be devoted to the expenditures procured due to field trips.

Preparation

- After planning, students and teachers should prepare for the trip.
- Should know the purpose of visit, the things that they should look, what things are to be collected, what type of information is to be recorded.
- Directions of activities.
- How to record.

Execution

- Teacher acts as a guide and supervisor
- Reaching the place, teacher must direct the students. Also see to it that all students follow the instruction.
- Draw student's attention to the important things and make certain that all the pupils participate and get the desired information.

Places of field trips

- Zoo
- Museum
- Bird sanctuary
- Dairies
- Hospitals
- Aquaculture farms
- Tea gardens
- Botanical gardens
- Green fields
- Forests
- Ponds, lakes, stream
- Fish farms
- Research laboratories
- Poultry farms
- Veterinary centres
- Sea shores
- Visit to polluted sites
- Tissue culture centres
- Vermiculture centres
- Nature parks
- National parks and sanctuaries
- Science exhibition and science fairs
- Population growth Centres

Advantages of field trip

- Every thing cannot be learnt in the classroom, hence excursions provide opportunities for direct experiences and thus learning becomes more accurate and meaningful.
- Provide first hand information to supplement and enrich classroom Instructions.

- Co-relate the school life with the outside world and community.
- Create situations, which develop a spirit of scientific enquiry.
- Application of learnt knowledge.
- Provide basis for a number of projects and study material.
- Pupils learn planning, co-operation, helping.
- Learn to discharge responsibilities.
- Arouses interest of students, and vitalizes instruction.
- Students' get opportunities to collect things and preserve them.
- Provide recreational dimension to study.
- Students see the relation between science and society.

Disadvantages of field trip

School programme is disrupted

Field trips usually require at least a complete day or minimum 5 to 6 hours. This means that on such days no-classes will be held so the school timetable is disturbed. Also frequent field trips may cause lack of time for completion of the school syllabus.

Finance Problems

A field trip generally involves expenditures in name of transport.

Boarding and lodging and other expenses. Frequent field trips may burden the Accounting and balancing procedure of money matters in school. Also the students may be burdened to bear the expenses which may not be taken in a positive stride and prove to be troublesome for the students who are not financially secure.

Hazards and Accidents

- Hazard of taking class comprising of 30 – 50 or more pupils is great and this difficulty increases as age of the pupil's decreases.
- There is a great possibility of accidents and mishaps.

→ Is burdensome for Teachers or in-charge to control the students.

Few get full significance of the activity

→ If guides are untrained, and ineffective then purpose of trip fails.

→ Often the object of discussion is hidden from the view of large portion of pupils due to crowding and lack of room, hence they miss out both visual and auditory as well as hands on learning experience.

Establishment, i.e., many establishments are not equipped to handle large groups. So classes have to be broken into groups and so problems of supervision and handling.

Trips cannot be arranged at psychological time during unit, i.e., the establishments often find it inconvenient to permit a tour because of unavailability of finance, teachers/guides, time etc. So the relationship between unit and the related field trip is generally not possible.

Many Establishments propagandize rather than educate, i.e., generally establishments bring out sales simulation propaganda, thereby using the opportunity to advertise their product. So vital information is over shadowed.

Analyzing the content areas where field trips are possible

Std 11th (GSEB)

Chapter	*Place of visit*
→ **Classification of Plants**	→ Visit to Botanical Garden and Fields, forests and areas around pond, lakes eg. **e.g. Sasan Gir** → **Sayaji Museum** → **MSU-Botanical Garden** → **Harni Pond** → **Specimens of Botany museum**
→ **Classification of Animals**	→ Trip to Zoological museum, Zoos, Sanctuaries **e.g. Kamatibagg zoo** → **MSU-Zoology department**

→ **Evidences of Evolution**	Trip to Geologically based Institutes, museum **E.g. Geology dept of MSU for seeing Fossils like dinosaur eggs**
→ **Environmental Pollution**	Visit to places where Industrial Effluence in discharged, pollution control centres. <u>eg.</u> **Mini River near Mahi River** → **GIDC**
→ **Animal Breeding**	Trips to poultry farm, Fishing Industries, Apiculture and lac culture centres, silk Industries ocean and seashores. **e.g. Poultry farm near vermiculture centre at EME** **Pearl culture at Sikka (Jamnagar) Okha for Prawn culture** **Lingada for Aquaculture**

Std 12th (GSEB)

→ **Parts of a Flowering plant and Plant Adaptations**	Visit to Botanical Garden **e.g. Botanical Garden MSU**
→ Pollination and Fertilization	→ Gardens like Kamati Baag, Ajwa etc.
→ Natural resources management and Environment Impact	Trips to National Parks, Sanctuaries, Marine National Parks. e.g. Gir Forest Nal-Sarovar
Bio energy and Biotechnology	Visit to Biogas plants, Agro-technology centres, Dairies, Pharma Industries, Bakery Industry, Vaccine Institute e.g. Baroda Dairy → Anand dairy → Biogas plant at Methan (Mehsana) → Geothermal station at Unai and Lasundra (Gujarat) → Wind farm at Okha, Mandvi, Veraval → Hydel power station at Ukai
Pollution	Polluted sites like Industries around Ankaleshwar

Science Club

What are science clubs?

- A science club can be termed as an organization which caters for the inculcation of scientific attitude, a genuine interest in science and scientific activities, supplements the work of classroom and laboratory and puts the syllabus on a practical basis.
- It may not be possible to cater for individual interests and needs in a routine science programme. But a science club is the place where the pupils can engage in their individual interests, it provides an equal opportunity to the pupils to express their creative abilities and fosters development of new ideas.
- Facilitates a environment which is most congenial for the expression of pupils talent and self expression of the utmost hidden talents.

Difference between Science Club and Classroom activities

- Classroom is formal and pupils are asked to do something whereas a club is informal and the pupils are free to choose their activities.
- Pupils in club work not to satisfy their teachers but themselves.
- Provides freedom whereas in a class, pupils have to be conformed to a strict system.

Principles of Science Club

- Learning by doing
- Learning by living.
- Given satisfaction to pupils natural curiosity to handle things, independent research, self-expression and developing potential to fullest.
- Provides an outlet for the pent up emotions of children and channelize their energies towards desirable goals.

Science club movement

Science Clubs first started in USA and USSR. Had a tremendous impact on the development of science education.

They usually started right from lower grade classes so as to catch students young and develop scientific interest in them.

Science club movement in India

- The importance of Science Club was recognized by Indian Government as early as 1957-58.
- The Govt. guided by NCERT gives a non-recurring grant of Rs 1200
- In 1962, the number of govt. aided science clubs was 500 which rose to about 900 by 1966-68 and the number has grown and is still growing over the years.
- In order to make the science clubs more effective, NCERT has organized some Science Club Sponsor's Workshop during last few years. In these workshops, some such activities were organized which were desired to be started in the science clubs.

Aims of science club

- ➢ To encourage individual and group activities in field of science.
- ➢ Inculcate scientific attitude and provide training in scientific method.
- ➢ Develop habit of reading extra, taking part in debates and essay writing.
- ➢ Habits of exploration and creative and inventive faculties are developed.
- ➢ Develop in pupils, a sense of healthy competition for a better cause.
- ➢ Keeping in touch with recent advances of science and their effect on human life.
- ➢ To develop keen eye for observation.
- ➢ Provide opportunity to develop individual skills.
- ➢ Enables to realize sciences world and application in day to day life.
- ➢ Creates interest and enthusiasm to pursue science as a hobby.

- To get club Affiliated to the District and Regional Science Club.
- To develop interest in scientific hobbies like making aquarium, vivarium, herbarium, chalk, ink, toilets, cosmetics, photography, soaps etc.
- Provide opportunity for training in leadership and self-expression.
- Motivate the study of scientific phases.
- Celebrating Scientific Days.
- Holding Interschool competitions like debate, poster, slogan, essay, demonstration, quiz, dramas, plays, elocution etc.
- Educational and vocational exploration and guidance.
- From social point, fostering school spirit and co-operation and permits the spirit of service.
- Building conscious responsibilities towards community.
- The informal and free attitude between teacher and student leads to more personal feeling and loyalty between pupil and teacher, which is desirable.

Activities of Science Club

- Holding discussions, meetings, and debates on scientific topics.
- Arranging excursions, field trips to places of scientific interest.
- Holding science exhibitions and fairs annually.
- Prepare charts, models, diagram and also soap, ink, boot polish, cream, etc.
- Arranging lectures of eminent experts of science field.
- Improvise apparatus or collect specimens for science museum, such as plant, insects, rocks, or other materials.
- To render school services or community services in aspect of health and sanitation and calamities like earthquake, floods, etc.
- Celebrating science days.
- Dramatization on science themes.

- Making and maintaining aquarium, vivarium.
- Holding poster, chart, model making competition etc. along with slogan writing and essays.
- Reading reports or papers of scientific value.
- Preparation of scrap book, albums, Herbarium etc.
- Teaching photography, electroplating, slide making etc.
- Giving vocational guidance in science stream.
- Demonstrations such as first aid by doctor, fire extinguishing, earthquake relief and safety, safety in handling gas, electricity etc.
- Stress management through yoga, meditation and healthy habits.
- Making a school biological garden.
- Inter school competitions.
- Arranging extension lectures of the persons of science.

How to organize a science club?

1. Accommodation and Facilities

- Such as room which is specially for the science club in school set up.
- Proper Seating arrangement and provision for storage of materials.
- Adequate tools and equipments, e.g., for soap making, ink, equipments, chemicals, cosmetics etc.
- Provision for hanging charts, bulletin board, glass cupboards, for display, charts of do's and dont's members, annual programme, etc. Aids on displays such as models, specimens, etc.
- T.V. if possible along with V.C.R. to watch scientifically oriented programmes.

2. Type

That whether a general science club covering a range of scientific interest, open for all categories of students or a specific clubs restricted to specific areas such as Nature Clubs, biology club, etc.

3. Size

That is number of members in the club, office bearers, incharges, etc.

This also depends on the accommodation facilities

4. Selection of members and office bearers

5. Date and place for club meetings

Constitution of a Science Club

- ➢ Every science club should have a constitution and every member should strictly abide by it.
- ➢ Science club should form 2 types of bodies
  - General body
  - Executive Committee

General Body

- ➢ Consist of all students, head of Institution as patron, teacher in charge and the sponsor.
- ➢ **Members** may also be of 2 types:-

Ordinary members who pay subscriptions at the rate fixed by club.

- Active members – who take keen interest in club and actually work with the apparatus and equipment.

However the membership fees should not be strictly imposed on the students. It should be voluntary and open for all kinds of students.

- ➢ A normal fees should be charged and the club should also try to tap other sources also. Constitution of the club must include decisions and directions about the following:-

(1) Name of club and its aims.
(2) Conditions and procedures of becoming a member.
(3) Means to finance the club membership fees or other sources.
(4) Number, timing of meeting to be held during a session.
(5) Types of activities of be undertaken.
(6) How office bearers are to be selected, election procedure, fill up of vacant post, duties of each post etc.
(7) How members if not fulfilling duties are to be expelled.

Role of Teacher in Science Club

- Is the most important force and the success or failure of club depends upon how much enthusiasm, resourcefulness and ingenuity a teacher possesses.
- Is the pivot of all activities.
- Guides, motivates students.
- Is the planner, facilitator, co-ordinator and organizer.
- Has to be enthusiastic, zealful and energetic

Are Teachers enthused to run a science club

- In present state of affairs, teachers are not enthused for a science club because mostly time spent on club is not accountable and teacher gets mostly no credit. In this way it is mostly a burden for Teachers who are already overloaded.
- Authorities do not provide adequate facilities to Teachers and there is no provision for time for science club in the Timetable.
- This calls for sometimes sacrifices on part of Teachers.

Curriculum and science club activities Std 11th

1. Cell	Making slides of cells, Types of cell, charts of cells and cell division.
2. Cell division	Model of cells.
3. Taxonomy	Visit to zoological and Botanical garden. Collecting specimens, Mounting and preserving specimens. Making a science museum.
4. Virus and Bacteria	Visit to hospital and disease affected areas - debates and discussions on diseases - Awareness programme for diseases. - Lectures of Doctors and health Dept personnel's.
5. Classification of Plants and Animals	- making Herbarium, scrap books - setting up vivariums, museums, aquariums etc. - collecting specimens - visit to zoos, farms, botanical gardens etc.

6. Evidences of Evolution	- Preparation of charts, models etc.
7. Heredity	- Making survey of probability of hereditary characters - Understanding and holding general discussions on diseases and how to present them.
8. Pollution	- Posters, field trips to polluted sites, awareness campaigns, street plays, planting trees, celebrating days.
9. Population growth and control.	- Organizing talks, debates

Science Museum

How Science Museums Started

- The interest in science museums in India started some time in late fifties.
- First science museum was known as Birla Industrial and Technological Museum, Calcutta, established in 1959 by Government of India under CSIR.
  1965 - Visvesvarays Industrial and Technological museum – Bangalore.
  1977- Nehru Science Centre, Bombay.
- These museums besides having permanent galleries, also organize various activities such as mobile science exhibitions and fairs, science demonstration lecture, training programmes etc.

Museums in School

- It is desirable that every school should have a science museum of its own.
- Making a museum with the help of pupils is an interesting and motivating task.
- Teachers should encourage the pupils to collect materials and apparatus.
- Materials from different branches can be collected and this should be result of the co-operative and active endeavor of the teacher and the students.

A school museum will have number of things, the students when they go on various filed trip whatever specimen they have brought and preserved can be kept in the museum. We can have collection of rare herbariums in the museum, we can have various models and teaching aids prepared by students as part of their project works. We can also have dioramas in the museum, where the actual landscape of a particular time and the animals living than could be recreated in the glass box. Such dioramas are interesting study materials, the model within the glass box is made up of clay and plaster of paris. After it dries it is coloured to give the most natural look. Many specimens, corals, mushrooms can also be preserved, we can also have lichens in the museum.

Labeling the Exhibits

- Under each exhibit, there should be a label.
- Label should contain:
  (1) The name of the article
  (2) The family to which specimen belongs
  (3) Place from where collected
  (4) Name of person who gave it
  (5) Time and season.
  (6) Purpose
  (7) Brief description.

Importance of Museums

- Plays an important part in intellectual and cultural life of individuals.
- Generates sense of curiosity.
- The sense of beauty to see and appreciate the beauty of nature.
- The spirit of inquiry at the complexity of nature.
- The skill of man in using nature's resources for his own betterment.
- Helps to learn and relate to the content.
- Makes learning fast and easy to retrieve.

Garden

Biological garden can add great aesthetic value and educational value to any school. In the compound of school instead of having a concrete wall one can have fencing and hedge. Most of the schools have pillars with the help of moss stick climbers can be made to climb on such pillars which can have beautiful flower. The compound wall can also be made of various trees, which have medicinal importance. The carpet area of school should be covered with lawn and other beautiful seasonal plants. There should be areas of seed bed where the gardener and the science teacher can demonstrate to the students the process of germination, care to be taken of plants, addition of fertilizer, diseases in plants, symptoms of the diseases, economic value of plants etc. Groups of students can be asked to turn by turn look after the plants in the campus, they can also empty their water bags in the various plants for which they owe responsibility before going to home. Thus as teachers we will be able to inculcate some positive values among them regarding care for nature.

- A convenient site should be selected within the school compound for laying a biological garden to contain various types of local plants and rare plants.
- Should also have a small pond in a corner where small animals such as toad, frogs, fishes, rats, rabbits, birds etc can be reared.
- Various types of flowers and vegetables can be grown and pupils trained in taking care of them.

Aquarium

How to set up an aquarium?

Starting and maintaining a fresh water aquarium in the school laboratory is easily accomplished by any one who is willing to devote a little thought and care to the work. The pleasure and practical teaching advantages to be derived from one or more aquaria containing interesting plants and animal specimens is well work from the time and effort expended.

Before starting the aquarium, make sure that you have correct type of tank, right quantities of aquatic plant and animals keep in mind the basic requirements of the specimens to be included in such a demonstration, because a freshwater aquarium is a biological association of plant and animal life.

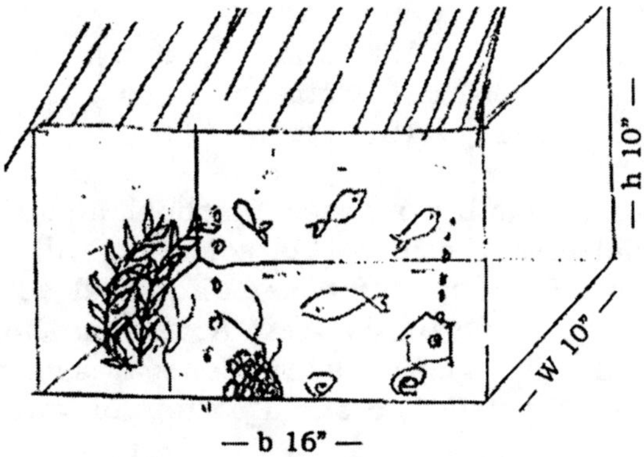

Picture 14. Aquarium.

Equipment

Absolutely, essential piece of equipment is a suitable aquarium tank. A rectangular tank with metal frame, glass ends and sides of about 6 to 9 gallon capacity is recommended. Small round aquaria are not satisfactory (visibility is poor through curved glass) and round fish globes are useless. In addition to a suitable tank, the following items prove their usefulness: dip net for transferring fish, one pair of long aquarium forceps, one pair of plant snips and a siphon tube.

Size of aquarium tank

It can be formed from aluminums as iron angles.

	Size	*Glass size* *Thickness*	*No.*	*Angle size*
1)	18″ × 10″ × 10″	18″ × 10″ 4mm	one	¾″ × ¾″
	L W H	18″ × 10″ 3mm.	two	
		10″ × 10″ 3mm	two	
2)	24″×12″×12″	24″ × 12″ 4mm	one	1″ × 1″
		24″ × 12″ 3mm	two	
		12″ × 12″ 3mm	two	

	Size	Glass	Number	Angle
3)	30″×12″×15″	30″ × 12″ 4mm	one	1″ × 1″
		30″ × 15″ 3mm	two	
		15″ × 12″ 3mm	two	
4)	36″×15″×15″	36″ × 15″ 4mm	one	1″ × 1″
		36″ × 15″ 3mm	two	
		15″ × 15″ 3mm	two	

On basis of availability of space in school, aquarium size can be selected. Besides this selection will also depend on circumstances such as funds and actual purpose for which aquarium is used. Aquarium should not be in orthodox fish globe shape because it is narrow at the top, so comparatively a small portion of water is exposed to air.

Other requirements

- Aquarium stand as per the size of aquarium tank
- Aquarium light-hood is necessary; fix the tubelight or bulbs in the hood.
- Aerator (Air pump) – one
- Plastic tuber plastic joints clamps as per requirements.
- Sand and gravel for aquarium base.
- Aquatic plants
- Different types of coloured fishes.

How to start freshwater aquarium?

- Clean the tank thoroughly, removing all dust, grease etc. from the glass. If the tank has previously been used as an aquarium, wash very thoroughly with soap and ammonia water. Rinse with clear water three or four times.
- Clean thoroughly in running water, sufficient aquarium sand and gravel to cover the bottom of the tank to a depth of one to two inches. Continue washing until all debris soluble matter has been removed. Place the sand in aquarium.
- Now keep some pebbles as large stones so that hiding places may be constructed and anchorage provided for those animals whose light bodies float

unless a firm hold is taken of some submerged objects.

- Now add the water. Use clear pond water if possible. If this cannot be obtained use tap water, which has stood in open containers for a day or so. Pour the water into the aquarium by laying a sheet of paper over it, up to 6 or 8 inches deep. After it has been planted add more water to fill the aquarium (NOTE: - Chlorinated city water is not safe to use unless it is allowed to stand in open containers for 48 hours).
- Aquarium should be placed where it will be exposed to strong diffused light. Direct sunlight for an hour as so each day is usually neither harmful in or it is necessary. North and east exposures are usually best.
- Aquarium can have variety of plants, as it is necessary for certain functions. Plants provide a natural habitat and protection for small fisher. Plants utilize some of the excreta thrown off by fish and other animals while, they, in turn are used as food by some species of fish and snails. They also promote the growth of microorganisms and other small animals.
- It is well to use plants rather sparingly at first because they soon grow and spread. If too many are crowded in the beginning, some may die and decay, thereby fouling the water. All plants will not thrive in an aquarium and it is best to secure tank grown (not wild) aquatic plants that can grow well in aquaria, e.g., Vallisneria, Sagittaria, Hydrilla, etc. Cobomba, Naias flexilis, etc.
- Planting in aquarium should be done by bending lower ends of plants with lead piece or stone, then fix the plants on bottom under the sand as gravel layer. Dead leaves or broken parts of plant should be removed periodically.

If the conditions are right, growth should be noticeable in about two weeks of planting. If the water does not become clear in a day as so it is usually an indication that it contains some dead and decaying plants, or other organic matter.

- Allow the aquarium to stand for few days until the water has cleared, when it will be ready for its animal population. Snails, fishes, etc. can be placed in the aquarium immediately after planting if necessary, but it is best to wait until water is clear.
- In stocking an aquarium several things must be taken into consideration. (1) Use only animals, which get along together, predaceous forms must be kept by themselves. (2) Do not use animals (or plants) which naturally live only in running water, as they will not live in the close confinement of an aquarium. (3) Do not overcrowd. (4) Do not use animals, which will stir up the sand on the bottom and the water cloudy.
- It is important not to overcrowd an aquarium with fish a good rule to follow is one inch of fish to one gallon of water. The average 6 gallon tank will support 6 one-inch fish or three 2 inch fish. The number of fish used must be governed by number of other animals to be included in the aquarium and the surface area of the water. It is usually advisable to use several small fish rather than one large fish small native fishes like minnows, bullheads, dace, sunfish, and guppies are more interesting than sluggish goldfish. If fish are not obtainable, snails, newts and aquatic insects will add much life and interest to the aquarium.
- 6 to 10 snails may be kept in a 6 – gallon aquarium. Snails are valuable as scavengers and will help to keep away algae from glass.
- Aquarium should be watched periodically and dead animal or dead parts of plants should be removed immediately. After the plants have become established it may be necessary to remove some of them to prevent overcrowding.
- Aquarium should be equipped with a cover. Any ordinary double or triple strength glass cut to the

right size, will answer the purpose. The cover serves a three-fold purpose, to prevent the entry of dust and debris, to keep the temperature of water from changing rapidly and lastly to reduce evaporation.

Feeding the Aquarium Fish

Two types of food (1) live food (2) dry food. Live food consists of crustaceans (Daphnia or Cyclops), earthworms, mosquito larvae, etc. Feed the fishes twice or thrice a week or an alternate day feeding is suggested live food helps in growth of fish.

Dry food is available in market, which consists of all required nutrition for fishes. It is advisable to provide dry food as it is cheap and promote the growth of fishes.

Occasionally aquarium should be checked. If water becomes foul, half the water should be taken out and fresh water should be added. Unconsumed food should be removed immediately.

In class, whole class can be divided into group of 5-8 students, which will taken care of aquarium. As a result all the students will get opportunity to have the experience with such type of artificial aquatic ecosystem.

Activities for Aquarium

- ➤ Drop of Aquarium water will show different aquatic living organisms like planktons, etc. under the microscope.
- ➤ Aquarium may serve as a source for obtaining mosquito larvae for observations on their structure, behavior, and life history and breathing activities.
- ➤ Observations on pond snail.
- - Feeding habits can be observed.
- - Snail movement can be observed, i.e., its behaviour. It moves sticking to the walls of aquarium.
- - Breathing – Snail comes to water surface for breathing. The mechanism of this way may form

topic for discussion. Respiration rate can also be taken by observing the animal's movement towards surface. It can be counted by taking particular time interval.

- Snail lay eggs in summer on any substratum in the aquarium. They form gelatinous mass of about 30 eggs each and approximately within one month they hatch out. The young developing snail can often be seen through eggshell under a microscope.

➢ Observations on fish.

- External features about eyes, skin, fish, gills and mouth as well as feeding and breathing habit may be observed.
- Scale of fish can be observed by removing it from skin with the help of pair of forceps.
- Observations on what happens when marine fish is kept in freshwater and fresh water fish in saltish water may be made. The recorded observation can be taken as topic of discussion.
- Development of fish from its egg may be observed.
- Various stages of development can be observed.

➢ Analysis of water in the aquarium.
By titration, chlorine content, magnesium content, turbidity of water can be estimated.

➢ Study of various aquatic weeds can be done by having weeds like hydrilla, Vallisneria, etc. in the aquarium.

➢ Study of various ornamental fishes having different colours and characteristics can be studied. Certain fishes having peculiarities can also be studied.

➢ Effect of pollution on fishes can be studied as they have difficulty in respiration in polluted water. Respiration rate increases in polluted water.

➢ Aquarium can serve as a ready source of material for experiment on water plant like photosynthesis, transpiration, etc.

➢ Algae like spirogyra, chara, etc can be observed on their cell structure in living condition.

- These experiments can be further extended and life at first hand is studied at a pond situated preferably within school premises.

Advantages of Aquarium

- Aquarium serves as a 'live corner' in the school where animals and plants are grown and reared.
- Students are able to study interdependence of animals and plants and of animals on animals.
- Thus help to study food chain and food web in artificial aquatic ecosystem.
- These types of activities in school open new avenues of enjoyment and interest. Thus, enhancing the development of affective domain.
- It develops keep eye for observation and various psychomotor skills are developed through handling of live plants and animals.

Disadvantages of Aquarium

- It is very much time consuming activity in consideration with tight schedule of school.
- Resources may not be available in terms of glass made aquarium, space requirement, aerator, etc. It would be found costly to accommodate in our syllabus as per the condition of Indian Schools.
- Students may not be so experienced to handle the live animals and proper care to be taken for maintenance of aquarium. This may cause unnecessary death of living organisms.

Curriculum and Activities

12th Std

1. Molecules of living Organisms -1- Water and Minerals	➤ Effects of freshwater and marine water on fishes, Experiments of turbidity, salinity. Biological oxidation demand, chemical oxidation demand.
2. Plant tissues	➤ Study of tissues in aquatic plant and their organization.
3. Development in flowering plants	➤ How water pollination occur
4. Animal tissues	➤ Dissections to study of anatomy of animals.

5. Genetics	➤ Hybridization, Inheritance, variation.
6. Ecosystem	➤ Study of aquatic ecosystem food chain and food web.
7. Biotechnology	➤ Genetic engineering, Development of fish food
8. Pollution	➤ Effects of pollution on fishes.

11th Std

1. Cell ➤	➤Different types of cells in aquatic plants.
2. Classification	➤ Aquatic plants and animals, classification.
3. Living Organisms and Environment.	➤Effect of biotic and abiotic components in artificial ecosystem, food chain and Food Web.
4. Environmental pollution	➤ Water pollution – Effects on aquatic ecosystem.
5. Plant breeding, Animal breeding	➤Studying about freshwater and marine fishes.

Herbarium

What is Herbarium?

In the literal sense herbarium means a collection of herbs, meaning plants. Technically speaking, it is a storehouse of dried specimens of plants arranged according to particular system of classification.

What is the need for making herbarium?

Herbarium is a handy means of plant identification, which is basic to all researches connected with plant and plant products. So aim of herbarium is to present a picture by means of representative specimens, of the composition of present flora. It forms the basis for future studies.

Activity of plant identification and nomenclature is carried out with the help of herbaria. So classification in plants can be studied through herbarium.

Besides this, specimens collected from all over world can be incorporated in herbarium, which will represent world flora.

An advantage of plants is that they can be preserved almost indefinitely in the form of dried specimens. So herbarium enables storing of large numbers of specimens in comparatively limited space.

Steps involved in herbarium making technique

Herbarium technique involves (i) collection (ii) drying (iii) poisoning (iv) mounting stitching (v) labeling.

(i) **Collection**: Collection of plant material for the herbarium should be done using aesthetic sense and scientific mind. One who collects must know what is to be collected. Indiscriminate collection may often prove to be worthless.

Specimens collected should be representative of species. Small herbs should be collected as entire plants, may be in large number since many can be made into a single herbarium sheet. In case of trees as shrubs only small twigs can be collected but they should be representative, bearing several leaves, buds, open flowers and fruits. Fruits and seeds may be gathered separately and attached to herbarium sheet later.

Only health specimens devoid of defects by attack of pests and diseases should be collected. They should also be free of eggs and larvae of insects, which may not be easily noticed. One method suggested to eradicate pests and parasites is immersing the specimens in 4% formalin before putting in the press.

Relevant information in respect of all aspects needed for determination of number of species collected, area from which it is collected, etc. can be noted in field note-book. This should include notes no habit, habitat, flower colour, locality, altitude and other interesting features which cannot be preserved on herbarium sheets.

(ii) **Drying:** Plant body contains plenty of water. If this water is not completely removed plant body will decay. Plant body usually becomes crinkled and deformed when it dries up. Such material will not reveal all morphological features. So this problem can be overcome by drying plants under high pressure. Even the most delicate parts of plant are not destroyed by pressure, though their 3 dimensional shapes may be altered.

There is an equipment called 'Portable Plant Press' through which fresh specimens are pressed flat, without folds and dry quickly. Standard size of plant press is 12X18 inches. A good portable press consists of two metallic frames holding thick mesh of galvanized iron and arrangement to tie the two frames in adjustable belts. Between the metallic frames are kept drying sheet of blotting paper and between the blotters are kept folded newsprint sheets (wrappers), in each of which collector places onc kind of plant. After keeping specimens in the newspaper folders, two frames are securely fastened by straps.

When preparing press, care should be taken to see that surface of stacked specimens present a flat surface so that pressure applied is equally distributed. For this, slightly change the positions of successive specimens in the press. Plant press holding pressed specimens can be kept in sun or suspended over moderate heat. After 24 hours, open the press and replace now wet papers with fresh dry ones. First 24 hours form 'sweating time' after which specimens are limp enough for proper placing. Paper should be changed at least once every day till specimens become perfectly dry. In moist weather, changing paper twice a day is recommended.

Sometimes flowers or other delicate parts may stick on to the drying paper and may be difficult to separate without damage. To prevent this, thin pad of tissue paper may be placed above and below such parts.

Aquatic plants dry up and disfigured very quickly, after removal from water. To avoid this, they should be placed between two drying sheets as soon as collected. Such wet sheets should be put into press only with adequate dry sheets above and below.

Submerged algae must be collected straight on the mounting sheet placed under water and transferring specimen on to it, so that their habit is altered the least. Then lift the sheet out of water avoiding disfiguration of specimen. Tissue paper should be placed over them when drying.

Quality of dried specimen largely depends on thickness of paper wads, frequency of changing and amount of pressure applied.

(iii) **Poisoning**: Specimens need poisoning to keep away insects and fungal pests. This is normally done when specimens are partially dehydrated, using chemicals such as corrosive sublimate 1% Mercuric chloride or any other suitable poisons. Specimens are again dried and kept ready for mounting.

(iv) **Mounting**: After the pressed specimens are fully dry, they are securely fastened to white card sheets. The standard size of herbarium sheet is 29×42cm. On the top of the Herbarium sheet, name of Herbarium is printed. On the lower right hand corner, some field and other data about the specimen must be given on a label. The process by which dried specimens are transferred to herbarium sheets is known as mounting.

Specimens may be mounted in various ways

- Specimens can be attached to the herbarium sheet by the use of strips of gummed cloth (known as Holland Cloth) supplemented by a non-staining glue which can be applied to the plant by means of spatula as by keeping specimen on a glued glass plate and then transferring it to the herbarium sheet.
- Glue may be applied straight to the specimen with soft brush and then specimen transferred to the mount.
- Specimen is *stitched* to the herbarium sheet by thread, using a needle and keeping knots on reverse side. This method is rather dangerous of specimen getting damaged during process of stitching.

During drying as well as while storing dried specimens, insect repellents and fungicides will have to be applied to prevent damage to specimens.

(v) **Labeling**: The heads under which information is required is either printed on right side of the bottom of sheet or is printed on labels (about 3×5 inches size) which can be pasted on the right bottom corner of the herbarium sheet. It should include at least the following information:

(1) Genus, species and family.
(2) Exact place of collection i.e. country, province, district and exact spot of collection.
(3) The habitat.
(4) The date of collection.
(5) Name of collector.
(6) Collector's field number.
(7) Name of person who identified specimen, if not the collector.
(8) Other information.
   - Colour of flower.
   - Height of plant.
   - Local use of plant, if any.

Care of Specimens: A carefully dept specimen should last indefinitely. The greatest hazard to specimens is from microbial and insect at lacks. The specimens are usually sprayed with 2% solution of mercuric chloride in rectified spirit. Paradichlorobenzene or even commercial naphthalene balls should be kept inside the pigeonholes. Once in a year, specimens can be bulk fumigated by mean of carbon disulphide after keeping them in closed chambers or steel trunks.

Curriculum and Activities

12th Std.

Chapter	*Activities*
1. Introduction to organs of a typical flowering plant	➢ Study different types of roots, Study different parts of flower by taking L.S. of flower and mounting that in herbarium, e.g., hibiscus, etc. ➢ Herbarium of seed or fruit can be made but it should be kept for drying for 2-3 days before it is pressed, as they contain lot of water content, E.g., maize grain, bean seed. Etc.
2. Plant adaptations.	➢ Different shapes of leaves can be mounted in herbarium as they are modified for adapting to environment.

	➢ Similarly herbarium of root modification, stem modification can be made.
	➢ Certain plants have modification for climbing, protection, photosynthesis, vegetative propagation etc. Root modifications for breathing, parasitic, etc. So all these modified stems or roots can be studied through herbarium.
3. Development in flowering	➢ Herbarium of different stages of plant development can be made. i.e. from grain up till the whole plant has grown.
11th Std. 4. Classification of plants.	➢ Herbarium is actually made on basis of species. Plant collected should be characteristic of species, i.e., it should be representative of species showing all characters
5. Plant Breeding	➢ Different cereals, vegetables, spices plants, medicinal plants, plants for making Beverages (Tea, Coffee), etc. can be studied through herbarium. ➢ There can be collection of medicinal plant like Glycerihiza, Raulwalfia, Penicillin, Quinine, Ardushi, etc.

Does herbarium making affects nature?

Herbarium making does affects nature because every student collecting specimens for his/her herbarium destroys plants. It can't be overlooked that on one hand we are talking of preserving nature and on the other hand we are disturbing natural growth of plants for our studies.

On one side herbarium gives detailed information of particular species of plant but it completely destroys that plant.

So as a suggestion it can be stated that if 4-5 students can work for one herbarium, the destruction can be minimized.

In such type of activity, certain species may get extinct and specimen will only remain as specimen and no live plant exist for that species.

Terarium

What is a Terarium?

- Represent a complete land environment where by different plants and animals, which are terrestrial, are presented.

How to Set Terarium

- May be prepared like an aquarium.
- At bottom, a layer of sand and small stones be placed.
- Around the edge of the container, a band of moss may be placed.
- A handful of charcoal may be scattered over the sand layer to act as absorbent. Then it is covered with a few inches of moist loamy soil prepared by mixing soil or sand with decayed leaves.
- Over this, a few plants and animals are housed.
- For effectiveness, a few rocks and fungus bearing branches may be added.
- Small toads, lizards, insects and animals can be placed.
- Occasionally water terrarium.

Possible Terrarium in Schools

- Terrarium for Hedgehogs, rabbits, Guinea Pigs, Rats, dormice and other mice.
- Take cage of wood. One part of the box should be partitioned off for general retreat.
- A suitable opening must be made in the partition for easy communication between two compartments.
- In case of rats and mice which breed freely, more than one generation can be kept in same cage.
- Guinea pigs and rabbits – kept in separate cages.

- Hedgehogs and dormice – cages must be of thick boards and well joined.
- Provide a liberal supply of sawdust, which is absorbent mix disinfectant power also with, saw dust.
- Provide opportunities for climbing, stairs, galleries or branched brows of trees wedged firmly into the cage.

Advantages of Terrarium

- Serves as a good instructional medium.
- Is interesting, attractive and cheap.
- Contribute to learning various concepts of plants and animals on land surface.
- Permits a greater variation in the types of environment to be illustrated.

Types

- May be prepared to represent a bag type terrarium showing how plants and animals live in wet places.
- May represent plants and animals live in not dry lands?
- May contain certain plants and animals living at different elevations on the surface of land.

Role of Students in Terrarium

- Students are the ones who are most responsible for setting up and the maintenance of terrarium.
- Groups of students must be made to take care of terrarium.
- Sharing of responsibilities like cleaning the terrarium, providing food and water, and making food, checking the animals health, applying antiseptic, proper lightning.
- Maintaining a record of the maintenance of the animals.
- Labeling their cages with name, classification, age, status, etc.

VIVARIUM

- Is a live corner where flying animals like birds and insects are kept?
- Is very much similar to an aquarium.

How to make Vivarium

- Take suitable receptacles like a set of flat glass topped tins about 2-3 inches in diameter.
- Usually rectangular tins make better vivarium but have joints through which the animals can escapc so round ones are preferred.
- These tins can be fitted with a layer of plaster of paris, which retains moisture without being wet.
- A small piece of blotting paper can also be kept.
- The insects kept may be provided with food like bread, leaves, aphids, seedling etc.
- The tin must contain sufficient and fresh food when necessary, as it is apt to spoil quickly.
- Caterpillars, which undergo metamorphosis phases, must be provided with fresh food plant, which is put in bottle filled with water.
- Humble bees and wasps – put few flat flowers like ox – eye daisies in small bottle of water and put in glass case in which honey bees have been put. Put a mixture of honey and water on these hovering around the watch glasses containing the same.
- For birds – in the school a large cages or room sized cage made of wire net can be made in the premises.
- Here different kinds of birds can be stocked.
- Provided natural environment like if possible trees, plants, nests, shelter, food and water provisions saw dust, etc.

Advantages of Vivarium

- To model the activities in school on the affairs of real life.

- Relate topics to real life experience, e.g., metamorphosis of bees, wasps, rearing of insects, habit, habitat, knowing the behavioural pattern, etc.
- Knowing the variety of birds and insects, their classification, habit, habitat etc.
- Is a source of enjoyment and recreation of plants and animals?
- Builds co-operation, unity etc in pupils.
- Creates a sense of responsibility among students while taking care of animals.
- Learning is more effective and fruitful see the bounties of nature and appreciates it.

12
Evaluation in Biology

Any good task comes to an end. So is the case for this book. Having seen variety of things we have come to the last and the very crucial chapter evaluation. Evaluation is the process of checking how far the objectives have been achieved. It is a continuous and comprehensive evaluation. It is formative as well as summative.

In Biology we have many activities that require evaluation.

Presentation:: In Biology students make various presentation in the discussion method (discussion of unknown topic), this may be individual or group. The presentation has to be evaluated by using some criteria. It can also be used to evaluate the project presentation.

Criteria for Evaluation of Presentation

Sr. no.	*Criteria*	*Percentage*
1.	Clarity of ideas	30%
2.	Pronunciation and proper punctuation	10%
3.	Self Confidence	10%
4.	Voice loud and clear	20%
5	Use of some aid OHP/Chart/ PowerPoint	20%
6.	Team Effort	10%

If the presentation is individual then 10% can be added to self-confidence.

Process of evaluation: before the presentation the criteria for evaluation should be given to all students. The weightage can also be explained to students. All the students can make their columns and write the percentage. Teachers can also separately grade the students. Finally one can give the pooled average to the pupils.

Discussion: The presentation must be followed by discussion. Presentation and discussion are unique learning forums for further concretization of highly abstract ideas. Evaluation of discussion requires a moderator. The questions must be sent to the moderator. The queries must then be answered by the participants.

Criteria for evaluating a discussion

Sr.	*Criteria*	*Percentage*
1.	Appropriateness of questions asked	30%
2.	Frequency of questions asked	30%
3.	Frequency of questions answered	30%
4.	Maintenance of decorem	10%

Process of Evaluation: Roll number sheets can be generated and in front of the roll number tally marks may be placed to indicate the participation in asking questions, some symbol can be used for appropriateness of questions and also to note frequency of answers.

		Symbol
Appropriate question	-	A
Frequency of question	-	|
Frequency of questions answered	-	*

A teacher can evolve his/her own ways of allotting symbols. Minimum two people must work on these roll number sheets.

Sample of roll number sheet for evaluation of discussion for ________ topic

Date: **Group/Project: Name/No.**

Roll number	*Symbol*	*Roll Number*	*Symbol*
1.		7.	
2.		8.	
3.		9.	
4.		10.	
5.		11.	
6.		12.	

Signature 1. ____________

Signature 2.____________

3. Exhibits / Audio Visual Aids/ Models

The students either prepare charts, static models or working models. These exhibits need to be evaluated objectively. That is different people at different place and time must be able to evaluate the students in the most appropriate framework without much deviation.

Chart: A chart must have border, must have a back support so that it does not turn or fly with fan. The magnification on chart must be depicted proportionately enlarged or condensed it must not happen that starfish and elephant look as if they were of same size.

Criteria for chart evaluation

Sr. No	*Criteria*	*Weightage*
1.	Drawing accuracy	30%
2.	Colour scheme	10%
3.	Concept clarity	20%
4.	Labeling	30%
5.	Support and hanging	10%

Chart should not be congested with too much of information

Models: The model can be static or working model. The model must be properly labeled as far as possible it should be self explanatory. Post card sized cards can be attached to them to make them further clear and self explanatory. If some thing is enlarged then its original size must be mentioned.

Evaluation Criteria for models

Sr. No.	*Criteria*	*Percentage*
1.	Exactness/originality	30%
2.	Self explanatory	25%
3.	Neatness/Skill	10%
4.	Colour	10%
5.	Viva-voce	25%

Exactness to see whether it resembles the original organism or not and to what extent. Self-explanatory as far as possible it must contain tags as labels for each part and arrows can indicate the process/ path.

Neatness model would require a lot of cutting pasting, fixing, colouring, labeling and drawing all this would need lot of neatness. Color scheme selection of colour is important to give that natural look to the model. Color gives the need precision to the model. Viva-voce is essential and important element of evaluation as teachers we cannot know how a student has worked on the model. Viva-voce could be used to focus on the questions related to the construction of the model.

Herbarium/ vivarium/ aquarium:

A. Herbarium: The Herbarium sheets have to be evaluated based on proper drying straight, neat fixing, disinfecting and proper labeling.

B. Vivarium: The vivarium can be evaluated by adding the maintenance and labeling dimensions a card about the classification collection and collector's name can be written on it.

C. Aquarium: The aquarium can be evaluated on the following criteria.

Construction 50%

Maintenance 50%

Assignment: They are given individually based on the objectives to be achieved by giving such assignments, they must be evaluated to understand how far the objectives are achieved by the self study of the given assignment. Some other criteria, could be clarity, precision, originality, conciseness, neatness, and neat labeled diagram.

Sr. No	*Criteria*	*Percentage*
1.	Clarity	20%
2.	Precision	20%
3.	Concise	20%
4.	Originality	15%
5.	Neatness	10%
6.	Neat labeled diagram	15%

Apart from the evaluation mentioned above there are two more evaluation.

Theory evaluation and practical Evaluation

First let us see theory evaluation

Basic ways of Describing Classroom Evaluation Procedure

Basis for classification	*Types of Evaluation maximum performance*	*Function of Evaluation what individuals can do when performing at their best.*	*Illustrative instruments. Aptitude, achievement tests.*
Nature of measurement	Typical performance	Determine what individuals will do under natural conditions	Aptitude, interest and personality inventories, observational techniques peer appraisals
Use in classroom instruction	Placement	Determines pre-requisite skills, degree of mastery of course objectives and/ or best mode of learning	Readiness tests, aptitude, pretests, self report, inventories, observation techniques.
	Formative	Determines learning progress provides feedback to reinforce learning and corrects learning errors.	Teacher made mastery test, custom made tests from test publishers, observation techniques
	Diagnostic	Determines causes intellectual, physical emotional, environmental of persistent learning difficulties	Published diagnostic test teacher made diagnostic test observation techniques.
	Summative	Determines end of course achievement for assigning grades or certifying mastery of objectives	Teacher made survey tests, performance rating scales, product scales.
Methods of interpreting results	Criterion referenced	Describes pupil performance according to a specified defined learning tasks (e.g., add single digit whole numbers)	Teacher made mastery test custom made tests from test publishers observational technique
	Norm referenced	Describes pupils performance according to relative position in some known group (e.g ranks 10th in a classroom group of 20)	Standardized aptitude and achievement test teacher made survey test, interest inventories adjustment inventories.

Mastery versus survey tests: Some achievement tests measure the degree of mastery of a limited set of specific learning outcomes whereas others measure a pupils general level of achievement over a broad range of outcomes. Mastery test typically use criterion referenced interpretation and survey tests tend to emphasize norm referenced interpretation, but some criterion –referenced interpretation also are possible with carefully prepared survey test.

Difference between Internal and External Assessment

Internal Assessment	*External Assessment*
Paper is set inside the school and also checked inside the school	Paper is set outside the school and is also checked outside the school
Students are more concerned about learning	Students are concerned more about passing exams
Feedback is given to the students immediately	Immediate feedback is not avail able to the students
Evaluation is a continuous and comprehensive process.	There is provision for year end examination
Internal evaluation focuses on the process dimension of teach-ing learning thus enhancing the quality of the on going process.	External exam results give exter-nal credentials to the school, though measured by external agency "we still are best". It give compares the school with other schools.

Norm referenced test (NRT) and Criterion referenced test (CRT)

One is to describe the performance in terms of the relative position held in some known group (e.g., types better than 90% of the class members). The other is directly to describe the specific performance that was demonstrated (e.g., typed 40 words per minute without error). The first is NRT second is CRT.

NRT provides pupils relative standing in the group

CRT provides percentage of correct score

Difference between Norm referenced test and Criterion referenced test

Sr. No.	*Norm Referenced Test*	*Criterion Referenced Test*
1.	Typically covers a large domain of learning tasks, with just a few items measuring each specific tasks	Typically focuses on a delimited domain of learning tasks, with a relatively large number of items measuring each specific task.
2.	Emphasizes discrimination among individuals in terms of relative level learning	Emphasizes description of what learning task individuals can and cannot perform.
3.	Favours items of average difficulty and typically omits easy items	Matches item difficulty to learning tasks, without altering items difficulty or omitting easy items.
4.	Used primarily (but not exclusively) for survey testing.	Used primarily (but not exclusively for mastery testing.
5.	Interpretation requires a clearly defined group.	Interpretation requires a clearly defined and delimited achievement domain.

Common in both

1. Both require specification of the achievement domain to be measured.
2. Both require a relevant and representative sample of test items.
3. Both use same type of test items.
4. Both use the same rules for item writing.
5. Both are judged by the same qualities of goodness (validity and reliability).
6. Both are useful in educational measurement.

Formative tests - Favours CRT because it is descriptive in nature.

Summative test - Favours NRT because it emphasizes norm referenced interpretation few item for each outcome.

Teacher Made Achievement test:

Preparation of Blue print

Weightage of Each Unit

Sr. No	Name of subunit	Weightage	Marks
1.	Concept of Natural Resources	10%	2
2.	Natural Cycles	20%	4
3.	Soil and its Conservation	35%	7
4.	Forest and its Conservation	23%	41/2
5.	Non renewable natural resources	12%	21/2
6.	Total	100%	20

Weightage to Objectives

Sr. no	Objectives	weightage	Marks
1.	Knowledge	28%	51/2
2.	Understanding	32%	61/2
3.	Application	25%	5
4.	Skill	15%	3
5.	Total	100%	20

Weightage to Different Items

Type of item	I	II	III	IV	V	Total number of items
Objectives	2+1 (1)(1)	2 (1)	2 (1)			7
Short question		1 (3)		1+1 (2)+(21/2)	1 (21/2)	4
Long question			1 (6)			1
Total item	3	3	3	2	1	12
Total marks	2	4	7	41/2	21/2	20

objectives	*Knowledge*			*Understand-Ing*			*Application*			*Skills*			*Total items*	*Marks*	*Percentage.*
unit	Ob.	S..A	L. A.	Ob.	S. A.	L. A.	Ob.	S. A.	L. A.	Ob.	S. A.	L. A.			
I	2+1 1 1												3	2	10 %
II	2 1										1 3		3	4	20 %
III	1 1/2			1 1/2		1 6							3	7	35 %
IV		1 2											2	41/2	23 %
V								1 21/2					1	21/2	12 %
Total item	6	1		2		1		2			1		12	-	-
Marks	31/2	2		1/2		6		5			3			20	100 %
Total Marks	51/2			61/2			5			3			-	-	-

Objectives of the Test

Concept of natural resources. 1. Students will be able to state the definition of natural resources in 1-2 lines

2. Students will be able to classify natural resources into its two types

Natural Cycle:

3. Students will be able to name different types of cycles.

4. Students will be able to explain flow of H_2O in nature in 2-3 lines

5. Students will be able to explain nitrogen cycle in 5-6 lines

6. Students will be able to draw nitrogen cycle.

Soil and its Conservation

7. Students will be able to give atleast two points of importance of soil.
8. Students will be able to give two causes of soil erosion.
9. Students will be able to state the importance of vegetation in preventing soil erosion in 3-4 lines.
10. Students will be able to give measures to prevent soil erosion.
11. Students will be able to give measures to increase the fertility of soil.

Forest and its Conservation

12. Students will be able to describe the importance of forest in 4-5 lines.
13. Students will be able to give names of species facing extinction.
14. Students will be able to describe the measures of conservation of forest in 4-5 lines.

Non renewable Natural Resources

15. Students will be able to state the importance of non renewable natural resources in 5-6 lines.
16. Students will be able to justify the need of conservation of non-renewable natural resources in 5-6 lines.
17. Students will be able to give 4-5 measures of non-renewable resqurces.

Items for Test:

1. Natural resources are needed to ______________ Life.
2. Natural Resources are ________ and ________ types.
3. Natural Resources must be __________ to sustain life.
4. Renewable natural resources can be replenished through______________.
5. Water is renewed through ____________.
6. Draw a neat labeled diagram of nitrogen cycle.

7. __________Element is replenished in soil by legume crops.

8. Vegetation helps in preventing __________.

9. What measures should be taken to maintain fertility of soil. Explain any one with illustration.

10. "National Parks should be setup" give reasons.

11. Name any four animals that may become extinct in near future.

12. Measures should be taken to prevent wastage of non-renewable natural resources.

Answers

1. Sustain
2. Renewable and non-Renewable
3. Conserved
4. Natural cycles
5. Water cycle
6. Picture 15. Nitrogen Cycle (on Next page)
7. Nitrogen
8. Soil erosion.

9. There should be rotation of crops, E.g., wheat and legume plant chemical fertilizers use should be reduced as they decrease natural fertility of soil, e.g., killing of earthworm. Natural fertilizers should be used, e.g., cow dung.

10. Forests are being destroyed for obtaining forest products and land for agriculture. As a result the organisms are deprived of their habitat. This disturbs the environment balance and so there is a serious decrease in number of forest animals. National parks help in bringing the equilibrium in environment in environment and also protect plants and animals. Hence national parks should be set up.

11. Snow leopard, gibbon, wooly wolf, lion, golden cat, golden langur, red panda. etc.

12. The non-renewable resources cannot be replenished rapidly. It takes millions of years to replenish. Looking to the rate at which we are using up these resources, it is probable that these resources may get exhausted in near future. Such non-renewable

resources must therefore be used carefully, so that they last for a reasonably long period. Hence measures should be taken to prevent wastage of non-renewable natural resources.

Evaluation of practical

Evaluation of practical is possible by observing the students while performing the practical.

1. **Assessment could be made of journal notes:** The students are supposed to prepare the journal in which they record all the experiments that they carryout in a given year. After every practical is over on the next day they get it checked by the teacher. At the year-end depending on the neatness and regularity of work some percentage of marks can be allotted for the purpose. The focus should be on individualized work, no copy should be allowed in completion of the journal. Journalling helps in developing the skills of observing and then drawing neatly plus labeling the diagrams.

2. **Observation book:** The observation book is another important tool in biology practicals here the students draw the sketches whatever they observe during the practical it is like current record. In journal the student presents the fair picture whereas in the observation book the students draw their observations which they get signed on the same day of the practical; the observation book becomes the basis of writing the journal. One would argue why do double work first in the observation and then in the journal. The answer is fairly simple one, repetition helps in mastering skills and journal may get dirty because we may use stain and water, we don't want our fair record to become dirty that is other reason for not using journal directly.

3. **The process dimension of the laboratory work:** The process dimension is most difficult to measure how much the students do and what process do they adopt to carryout the experiment. The process part tells us whether the students are careful observers or not, if they have observed the demonstration properly they

should not have much problem in carrying out the experiment but if there observation is weak they may miss a stage. Teacher must insist step by step procedure of carrying out the experiment. Because process is important to reach to the result, the process trains the students in scientific method and scientific attitude.

4. Product part of the laboratory work: At the end of the practical the students do get some result, may be the structure of stem or root, or dissection etc. Whatever be the nature of the practical the students do come up with some end result. Here the teacher can evaluate by seeing what process the student has followed and how he/she reached the result. Are the results satisfactory or not, which are the skills which are mastered and which skills require further mastery?

5. Conducting Viva Voce: Viva voce is the oral exam of practicals. The practicals integrate the theory and practical. In order to know how much integration has taken place in the students while learning a particular practical one needs to conduct oral examination. Here the questions pertaining to the theory of the practical can be asked to the students.

6. Handling of apparatus: In the biology practical the students are supposed to handle many apparatus, for e.g. microscope, dissection, microscope, forceps, brush, blade, scissors etc. How exactly the instruments are handled also requires to be graded by the teacher.

Some other factors are already discussed in the unit VII laboratory work.

For any test to be good it must have

Validity

Reliability

Objectivity

Usability

Steps involved in the construction of a test

1. Content analysis of the given content as on has taught. Keeping in mind the content analysis one prepares the objectives and also the learning experience to teach the students. So for

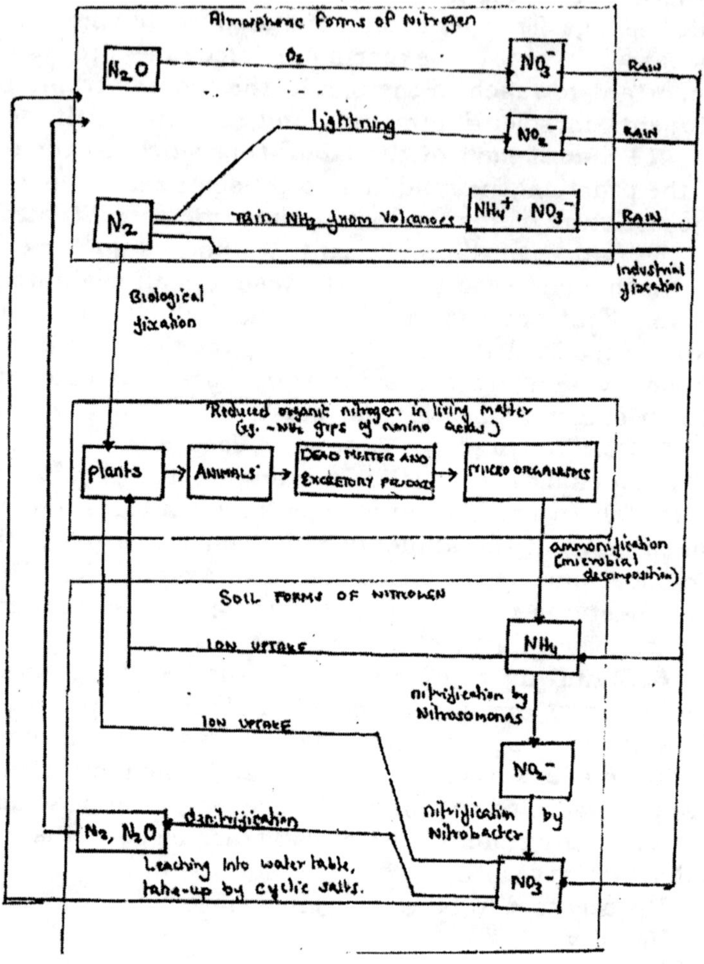

Nitrogen Cycle

evaluating the students also one must check the content analysis. Allocate proper weightage to the subunits.

2. Next stage would be to allocate weightage to the type of objectives. That is what percentage of items will be objective, short questions or long questions.
3. Combining objectives and the type of items prepare a question bank of all probable questions from a given unit. Here all type of items must be prepared for each unit. The question bank is very useful for a teacher, along with the question bank a teacher must also prepare a scoring key.
4. Third stage would be to select the type of items required for the current test. If it is diagnostic test items will be different, if it is remedial the items will be different so depending upon the nature of test different type of items can be selected from the question bank.
5. Prepare 3-dimensional blueprint. The three dimensional blueprint gives a clear-cut picture about level of objectives, type of questions, subunit and the marks allotted to each type.
6. Now prepare the question paper of the given blueprint by selecting appropriate items from the question bank. In preparing the question paper the average students must be kept in mind it should neither be for intelligent students nor for poor students.
7. Edit the question paper for proper language and clarity, also check the validity. The questions must be stated in a simple manner to avoid any confusion. The questions must be precise and concise.
8. Check that it can be finished in the stipulated time
9. See to it all instructions are clearly written. The instruction must include marks, time allotted, options should be written clearly. Total number of pages must be given.

10. Print the test. The printing should be legible to the students.
11. Administer the test. While administering if any instructions are to be given to the examiner they must be given.

Paper pencil test some factors to be kept in mind

This is the most popular teacher made test. The objective type test would include, Multiple choice, matching, true false, completion items.

General rules for making objective items.

- Keep the language simple: The attempt should not be to test the students vocabulary.
- Ask students to apply rather than simply recall information.
- Make sure that each item is independent. That is the answers are not available in the question paper itself.
- Do not establish a pattern for correct answers. For example every alternate item is true, such pattern should not bé there.
- Do not include trick or trivial question on tests as it reduces the reliability of test.

Principles for making Multiple choice

- Put as much of the item as possible into the stem. The stem of a multiple-choice question is that part which asks the question or states the problem. If the stem is written properly students get the idea as to what is asked.
- Make options reasonable: The options must have a discrimination value.
- Make sure unintentional clues are not provided.
- Homogeneity of the alternatives should be maintained.

True false items

- Be sure that each item is definitely true or definitely false.

- Avoid the use of all-inclusive or all exclusive terms.
- Be sure that items are not dependent upon insignificant facts.
- Be sure that true items are not consistently longer or shorter than false items.
- Avoid the use of double negatives and call attention to single negatives by underlining or capitalizing the negative word.
- Statement which are trivial in nature must be avoided
- Long and complex sentences must be avoided.
- Because as a result of such words must be avoided.

Matching items

- Limit the number of items to be matched to ten or less.
- Make sure all items concern one topic.
- Have more answers than questions or stipulate that some answers can be used more than once.
- Arrange options in some logical order.
- It should not run in two pages.
- To find relationship we go for matching items.
- The items should match.

Completion items

- Write items that can be completed with a single word or a short phrase.
- Be sure that only one word or phrase can correctly complete the sentence.
- Put the blanks near the end of the sentences.
- Make all the blanks of same length.
- Do not put more than two blanks in any one item.

Advantages of objective type items

- They provide a broad sampling of student's knowledge, as a large amount of content is covered.
- Present the same problems and the same alternatives to each student. That is the students are able to perceive the problem clearly.

- Minimize the chance of student bluffing, or spin a yarn.
- Can be scored quickly and with little, or no need for subjective decisions.
- Items can be improved on the basis of item analysis.
- Reliability can be increased through item improvement.

Disadvantages of objective type items

- Difficult to assess some cognitive skills as synthesis and creativity.
- Increases the possibility of guessing.
- Items take a relatively long time to construct.

Essay type items

They can be of two types short answer and long answer. In the short question answer students are expected to answer in one or two sentences. Whereas in the long answers the students are expected to write at length.

- Be definitive about what you want to ask, and what you expect from the students.
- Make sure students have sufficient time and materials to do the job.
- Grade papers as anonymously as possible.
- Compare each response to a model response or to a list of crucial points.
- When possible, have tests checked by more than one evaluator and average the grades.
- Internal options from the same unit and not different unit.
- As far as possible equal weightage should be given to all the units.
- Model answers must be provided which can be compared.
- Scoring key must be prepared.
- Questions should be grammatically correct.
- Model answers must also have alternate answers.
- Alternative illustrations must also be provided.

Advantages:

Emphasize high level cognitive skills, such as synthesis and evaluation

Provide an indepth sampling of student's knowledge of a specific topic.

Allow for student creativity, analysis, and synthesis skill assessment.

Easier to construct than objective tests.

Conclusion

Evaluation does many functions; diagnostic, remedial, summative, formative. It is helpful in analyzing how far the objectives are achieved. Evaluation also gives directions to teachers, students, principal and parents. The government can also know about the quality of education provided in the country.

All instructional procedures require evaluation some lend themselves to formal evaluation. Some procedures are more difficult to evaluate teachers here must rely on extent of students participation, degree of interest, a desire expressed by students for similar experiences.

Bibliography

- Anderson, L. W. (Ed.), Krathwohl, D.R. (Ed.), Airasian, PW., Cruikshank, K.A., Mayer, R.E., Pintrich, P.R. Raths, J., And Wittrock, m. C. (2001). "A Taxonomy for learning, teaching, and assessing: A revision of Bloom's Taxonomy : An Overview," *Theory into Practice*, 41 (4), 213-218.
- Bloom, B. S. (Ed.), Engelhart, M.D., Furst, E. J., Hill, W. H., And Krathwohl, D.R. (1956). "Taxonomy of Educational Objectives: The classification of educational Goals." *Handbook 1: Cognitive domain*,: David McKay., New York
- Das, R.C.(1985) *Science teaching in Schools* ; Sterling publishers Pvt. Ltd. New Delhi.
- Fink Arlene.,(1995). *Evaluation for Education and psychology* :Sage Publication, New Delhi.
- Grounland, Norman, (1968) *Constructing Achievement Tests*, Englewood Cliff, N. J. Prentice Hall, New Jersey.
- Grounlund, Norman E., (1970) *Stating Behavioural objectives for classroom instruction.* Toranto:Macmillan.
- Gupta, V. K., (1995) *Teaching and Learning of Science and Technology* published by Vikas publishing house pvt. Ltd. New Delhi.
- Harrow, A.J.(1972). *A taxonomy of the Psychomotor Domain: A guide for developing Behavioural objectives.* New York: David McKay.
- Heiss, E. D. et.·al. (1957) *Modern science teaching* Pub. by Macmillan Company New York.
- Joyce Bruce and Marsha Weils., *Models of Teaching* Prentice hall of India private limited New Delhi.

- Khan, M.I., Sharma, S. R., (1993) *Instructional Technology Media and theory,* Pub. by Kanishka Publishers Distributors New Delhi.
- Khirwadkar, Anjali., (2003) *Modern Methods of Teaching Chemistry,* Pub. by Sarup and Sons New Delhi.
- Krathwohl. David R., Benjamin S. Bloom, and Bertran B. Masia, (1964) *Taxonomy of educational objectives – The classification of Educational Goals, Handbook II: Affective Domain.* :David McKay, New York
- Lakhotia, S.C. (ed.), 2001. *Integrative Biology,* Indian National Science Academy, New Delhi, India
- Lakhotia, S.C., 1991. *Why "classical" is not classy?* Current Science 61: 708
- Lakhotia, S.C., 2000. Biology today: urgent need for an integrative approach. Current Science 78: 1414-1415
- Layton David (1971) *The Impact of science teaching,* published by oxford and IBH Publishing Co. New Delhi.
- Layton David (1987) *Innovations in science and technology education,* sterling pub. Pvt. Ltd. New Delhi.
- Marlow Ediger, Rao Digumurti Bhaskara (1996) *Science Curriculum* Discovery Publishing House New Delhi.
- NCERT (1965-66) *Organizing Science Clubs,* DESM, NCERT: New Delhi.
- NCERT (2000) *Biology,* Textbook for class XI published by Gujarat state board of Textbook , Gandhinagar.
- NCERT (2003) *Science and technology,* A textbook for class X published by NCERT, New Delhi.
- NCERT (2003) *Science And Technology,* Textbook for Class IX pub. by NCERT New Delhi.
- NCERT (2003). *Science,* Textbook for class VIII, pub. by NCERT New Delhi.
- NCERT. (1989) *Biology,* Textbook, standard XII part II, published by NCERT New Delhi.
- Pierce Walter, Lorber Michael., *Objectives and methods for Secondary Teaching.* Illinois State University: Prentice – Hall, Inc., New Jersey.

- Prasad, J. (1999). *Practical Aspects in Teaching of Science,* Kanishka Publishers Distributors, New Delhi.
- Rajput, J. S., V. P. Gupta, and Vaidya, N., (1978). *Survey of Science laboratories in the western Region.* Educational Trends, 13 (1): 91-99
- Rao Divakara Y. Gameti Divyesh S., *"Uniform Testing code in higher Education"* paper presented in UGC golden jubilee seminar, 2003.
- Rao U. K, Reddy, R. S. (1992) *The Nature of Educational Technology,* Pub. by commonwealth publishers New Delhi.
- Samanta, R.K. (1991) *Manual on instructional aids for teaching excellence.*
- Sharma, D. V. (1995) *Towards Quality secondary Education Agenda for 21st century Council of Boards of School Education in India,* (In association with Vikas Publishing House pvt. Ltd.
- Sharma, L. M. (1977) *Teaching of Science and life Sciences,* First Edition, Dhanpat Rai and Sons, Delhi.
- Sharma, R. C., (1995) *Modern Science Teaching,* pub by Dhanpat Rai and Sons, New Delhi.
- Sunil, Behari Mohanty(1987), *Methods of Teaching Science,* Books and books, Binod Behari, Cuttack.
- Unesco, (!963) *Source Book For Teaching Science,* UNESCO.
- Vaidya Narendra., *The impact of Science Teaching,* Oxford and IBH publishing company New Delhi.
- Vashist, S. R. (1993) *Perspectives in Curriculum Development,* Anmol Publications New Delhi.
- Yash Pal, Ashok Jain, Subodh Mahanti, (1993) *Science in society some perspectives,* Gyan Publishing House New Delhi.

Table 1. Web sites of major funding agencies, some research institutions and universities in India

Dept. Science and Technology (DST), Government of India, New Delhi.
http://mst.nic.in/dst

The University Grants Commission (UGC), New Delhi http://www.ugc.ac.in

Council of Scientific and Industrial Research (CSIR), New Delhi
http://www.csir.res.in

Board of Research in Nuclear Sciences (BRNS, DAE), Dept. Atomic Energy, Government of India, Mumbai http://www.barc.ernet.in/webpages/brns/brns1.html

Dept. Biotechnology (DBT), Government of India, New Delhi
http://www.dbtindia.org

Defense Research and Development Organization (DRDO), Government of India, New Delhi http://www.drdo.org/labs/dls/index.shtml

Indian Council of Medical Research (ICMR), New Delhi http://icmr.nic.in

Indian National Science Academy, New Delhi www.insa-india.org

Indian Academy of Sciences, Bangalore http://www.ias.ac.in ; http://www.iisc.ernet.in/academy

National Institute of Oceanography, Goa http://www.cmmacs.ernet.in/nal/icast/csir/nio.html

Wild Life Institute of India, Dehradun http://www.wii.gov.in

Tata Memorial Centre, Mumbai
www.tatamemorialcentre.com/research.htm

International Center for Genetic Engineering and Biotechnology, New Delhi
www.icgeb.res.in

Centre for Cellular and Molecular Biology, Hyderabad www.ccmbindia.org

Centre for Biochemical Technology, New Delhi
www.cbt.res.in

Tata Institute of Fundamental Research, Mumbai
www.tifr.res.in

National Centre for Biological Sciences, Bangalore
www.ncbs.res.in

National Centre for Cell Science, Pune
www.nccs.res.in

National Institute of Immunology, New Delhi
www.nii.res.in
Centre for DNA Fingerprinting and Diagnostics, Hyderabad
http://www.cdfd.org.in/
Bose Institute, Kolkata
www.boseinstitute.org
Indian Institute of Science, Bangalore
www.iisc.etnet.in
Department of Biological Sciences and Bioengineering, Indian Institute of Technology, Kanpur
www.iitk.ac.in/bsbe
Jawaharlal Nehru University, N. Delhi
www.jnu.ac.in
Hyderabad University, Hyderabad
www.uohyd.ernet.in
Delhi University, New Delhi
www.du.ac.in
Madurai Kamraj University, Madurai
http://www.dbtindia.nic.in/btis/dics/mku.htm
Pune University, Pune
www.unipune.ernet.in
Banaras Hindu University, Varanasi
www.bhu.ac.in
for a list of Universities in India
http://www.educationinfoindia.com

Websites of Biology related to Education:
members.aol.com/Cappuccinno21/BioWeb/webindex1.html - 5k – Cached - Similar pages
www.lib.uconn.edu/online/research/ bysubject/biokeywebsites.htm - 15k - Cached - Similar pages
www.utpb.edu/.../collegeofartscience/deptofsciencemathematics/ programofbiology/related_websites.htm - 11k - Cached - Similar pages
www.fife-education.org.uk/nof/ sector/Secondary/Biology.htm - 49k - Cached - Similar pages
teachline.ls.huji.ac.il/~general/textbooks-sites.htm - 63k - Cached - Similar pages

www.bbc.co.uk/learning/library/biology.shtml - 17k - Cached - Similar pages
www.accessexcellence.org/RC/biology.html - 9k - Cached - Similar pages
www.shambles.net/pages/students/Biology/ - 49k - Cached - Similar pages
www.lib.usf.edu/internetrefs/?s=bio - 35k - Cached - Similar pages
library.thinkquest.org/11771/english/ hi/biology/links.shtml - 14k - Cached - Similar pages
www3.district125.k12.il.us/science/ ACCBIO/accbiowebsites.html - 26k - Cached - Similar pages
www4.d25.k12.id.us/phs/teachersites/ - 30k - Cached - Similar pages
www.goongee.com/category.php?category=36 - 15k - Cached - Similar pages
www.nsta.org/main/sciencesites/default.asp?category=2 - 34k - Cached - Similar pages
www.nla.gov.au/pathways/jnls/austjnls/view/742.html - 8k - Cached - Similar pages
www.zoo.utoronto.ca/able/hotsites/hotsites.htm - 25k - Cached - Similar pages
www.splut.com/012/005.htm - 19k - Cached - Similar pages
[More results from www.splut.com]
library.stcc.edu/pathfinders/biology.htm - 5k - Cached - Similar pages
biology.st-and.ac.uk/websites.html - 26k - Cached - Similar pages
www.utyx.com/biology/plant-biology.html - 17k - Cached - Similar pages
www.baldegg.com/search/index.php/Science/Biology/ - 61k - Cached - Similar pages
www.spartacus.schoolnet.co.uk/internet41a.htm - 21k - Cached - Similar pages
infotree.library.ohiou.edu/byform:general/ health-and-life-sciences/biology/ - 11k - Cached - Similar pages
www.csupomona.edu/~library/websites/biology.html - 17k - Cached - Similar pages
[More results from www.csupomona.edu]

www.prayingeachday.org/3subeducationsites.htm - 23k - Cached - Similar pages
libweb.sonoma.edu/search/web/biology.html - 20k - Cached - Similar pages
shs.westport.k12.ct.us/mjvl/science/bioweb.htm - 41k - Cached - Similar pages
www.booksites.net/sub_discipline_pages/cws_sub_discipline/cws_biology.htm - 17k - Cached - Similar pages
www.microbiology.adelaide.edu.au/general/microwww.htm - 36k - Cached - Similar pages
serendip.brynmawr.edu/biology/b103/f98/websites.html - 12k - Cached - Similar pages
newarkbiosci.rutgers.edu/biology_websites.htm - 11k - Cached - Similar pages
alca.rutgers.edu/Bio100/SylF03loree.pdf - Similar pages
alca.rutgers.edu/Bio100/SylF03arc.pdf - Similar pages
library.simons-rock.edu/subjects/biology_ft.htm - 11k - Cached - Similar pages
www.uk250.co.uk/uk/search/for/biology/2 - 31k - Cached - Similar pages
[More results from www.uk250.co.uk]
www.library.veryhelpful.co.uk/Page%2019.htm - 8k - Cached - Similar pages
ecr.lausd.k12.ca.us/staff/fbeerstein/page12.html - 5k - Cached - Similar pages
www.rose-hulman.edu/users/groups/premed/Links.html
library.trinity.wa.edu.au/subjects/ science/biology/default.htm - 18k - Cached - Similar pages
www.khoj.com/Science_and_Technology/Biological_Sciences/Biology/ - 22k - Cached - Similar pages
www.emacmillan.com/our_projects.htm
www.indiastudycenter.com/studyguides/biology/
animals.about.com/cs/conservation/ - 21k - 10 Jan 2004 - Cached - Similar pages
imtech.res.in/raghava/biodiv/webpages.htm - 36k - Cached - Similar pages

www.directory.net/Science/Biology/
www.monsanto.com/monsanto/layout/sci_tech/
www.shambles.net/pages/students/Biology/
[More results from www.shambles.net]
www.education.nic.in/htmlweb/info.htm
www.directory.ultimate-resources.com/
www.ezresult.com/Regional/Asia/India/Education
www.iubs.org/test/bioint/43/7.htm
www.twis.org/science/education/
www.envirofinder.com/php/
www.dnheducation.net/local/news.htm
bluemoonworld.com/links/education-postsecondary.html - 101k - Cached - Similar pages
shikshanic.nic.in/cd50years/ar2002/chap9.pdf - Similar pages
www.mac.edu/academics/catalog/
www.teachernet.gov.uk/usefulsites/gtoj/
www.charm.net/~jblake/educat.htm
www.dec.org/pdf_docs/PNACS510.pdf

Index

A

Achievement indicators (big teaching), 31
Activity Aids, 202
Aesthetic value of biology, 45
Affective domain, 39
Affect Level Development test (laboratory), 162
Analysis (cognition), 37
Analysis Thinking Strategy, 147
Anderson, Kvathuohl et al, 39
Animal dissection, 32
Annual Planning, 55
  Advantages, 57
Annual Plan Formal, 56
Apparatus (Lab)
- entry in stock register, 159
- maintenance, 159-60

Applied Biology, 27
Application (in cognition), 37
Application/value of Biology, 44
Aquarium
- setting up, 222-27
- activities, 227
- advantages/disadvantages, 229
- use in class curriculum, 229

Articulation, 42
Assignment
- characteristics of good assignment, 80
- methods, 80
- merits/demerits, 83-84
- types, 81-82
- organisation, 82
- Activity centred, 81

Audio Material, 197
Audio Visual Aids difficulties/suggestions, 205
Automation, 43
Awareness of problems, 32

B

Banaras Hindu University
- new biology courses, 25

Behaviour Modification Model, 126
Biodiversity related topics, 26
Biology, 11
- teaching—present trends, 19-20
- branches, 27
- sustaining interest, 19
- correlation with other sciences, 49
- projects (India), 189
- curriculum modern trends, 185

Biology-Physical Sciences differences, 119
Biological Gardens, 221
Biological Sciences, 19
- future interest, 23

Biological Sciences Curriculum Study (BSCS), 185

- courses developed, 186
- Senior Secondary Biology Programme, 187
  - limitation, 188

Biological Research topics, 22
Biotechnology
- department, 23
- popularity, 24

Bloom, Benjamin
- levels of cognitive understanding, 34-35

Bloom's Taxonomy, 41
Brain Drain, 25
B.Sc. degree subjects in, 20

C

Charts, 196
Chemistry and Biology correlation, 50
Classical Biology, 27
Classroom environment, 130
Classroom Films, 199
Cognitive Understanding
- Bloom's study, 34-35
- categories, 36

Community trips, 203
Completion items, 257
Comprehension (in cognition), 36
Computer, 201
Concept types, 138
Concept Attainment Model (CAM)
- Goals and Assumption, 136
- processes, 136
- thinking strategies, 139

Concept Attainment, 136
- Teaching, 137
- Testing, 146

Concentric Method of Curriculum
- Organization, 181-82

Content Analysis, 53
Criterion Referenced Test (CRT), 246
and NRT difference, 247
Craft and Biology correlation, 51
Curriculum, 169
- development—styles, 183
- definition, 169-70
- modern concept, 171
- characteristics, 174
- variables of teaching, 172
- defects, 175
- expert advice, 173
- principles, 176-80
- purposes, 173
- approaches, 180
- organizing systems, 180

D

Deductive Approach, 103
Defence Research and Development Organization (DRDO), 23
Demonstration, 203
Demonstration Method, 93
- importance, 77
- merits, 79
- demerits, 79
- when used, 80

Department of Science and Technology (DST), 22
Diorama, 197
Disciplinary Approach of Curriculum Organisation, 180
Discussion Method, 93
- importance, 93-94
- procedure, 94
- after teacher has taught, 94
- of known topic, 94
- merits/demerits, 96
- role of teacher, 96

Documentary films, 191

E

Ecological Approach, 110
Enthusing factors in Biology, 26
Epidiascope, 198
Essay type items, 258
- principles, 258

Evaluation
- (cognition level), 38
- Planning, 60
- Instruments, 62
- in demonstration method, 79

Evaluation in Biology
- criteria, process, 241
- roll number, sheet sample, 242
- of exhibits, 243-44
- theory/practicals, 244
- of practicals, 252
- basic ways of classroom evaluation, 245

Excursions, 202
Exhibitions, 204
Eye (topic – teaching of) integrated approach, 113

F

Field Trips, 202
- types, 203
- arranging, 207-208
- preparation, 207
- finance, 208-209
- places, 210
- advantages/ disadvantages, 210-11
- class XI chapterwise, 212
- financial problems, 211
- hazards/accidents, 211

Films, 199
- for general information, 199
- for demonstration of skill, 199
- dramatizing an event or episode, 199
- methods of using, 200
- loops, 189

Fine Arts and Biology Correlation, 51
First Aid in labs, 155
- aim, 156

Flannel Board, 196
Flash Cards, 196
Flat Material (teaching aid), 196
Flora and Fauna study, 27
Folk Show, 202
Folk Theatre drama, play, 202
Formative tests, 247
Funding
- sources, 23
- agencies, 27-28

G

Garden (Biological), 221
Geography and Biology Correlation, 51
General Objectives of teaching biology, 33
Green Ecological Approach (BSCS), 186
Group Centred Method of Teaching, 69
Gujarat State
- biology option in schools, 20

H

Herbatian lesson plan, 62
- stages, 63
- presentation, 63-64

Herbarium, 230
- need, 230-31
- steps in making, 231
- collection/dressing, 231
- poisoning, mounting, labelling, 233
- specimen care, 234
- use in class XII, 234
- impact on nature, 235

Heuristic Method, 87
- procedure, 87
- role of teacher, 88
- merits, 89
- demerits, 89

Historical Method
- merits, 76
- demerits, 76
- topics which can be taught, 76

HSCE Board
- Marking Scheme, 196

I

Identification test in labs, 162
I I T Kanpur Dept of Bio Sciences/Engineering, 25
Indian Academy of Science – Bangalore, 25
Individual trips, 204
Inductive Approach, 100
- steps, 101
- merits/demerits, 103

Industrial Films, 199
Information Processing Model (IPM), 125
INSA Integrated Biology Programme (2000), 25
Inquiry, 105
- Approach, 104

Inquiry Training Model (ITM), 128
- Syntax, 129
- Limitations, 132

Instructional and Nurturant Effect, 128
- of ITMS, 132

Instructional experiences selecting, 59
Instructional intent, 43
Instructional objective, 33
- purpose, 33
- construction tips, 35

Instrumental Type of Curriculum, 184
Integrated Approach, 111
- in environment problem teaching, 111

Intellectual Values of Biology, 44
Internal/External Assessment
- difference, 246

Inter-school visits, 204
International Agencies initiating training and development, 27-28

K

Knowledge level of cognition, 36
Krathwohl, Bloom and Masia – objectives of teaching, 39

L

Laboratory Method, 84
- importance, 85
- steps, 85
- merits/demerits, 86
- role of teacher, 86

Laboratory
- planning, organizing and maintenance, 156
- infrastructure planning, 156, 158
- suggestions before constructing, 157
- equipment planning, 158
- organization, 159
- Administration, 159
- apparatus arrangement, 159
- maintenance, 160
- set-up diagram, 164-167

Laboratory Work
- assessment, 160-61
- objectives, 151
- types, 151
- preparing for, 152
- directions, discussion post Lab, 153

- safety measures, 154
- accidents/remedies, 154
- first aid, 155
- manipulative and observation Test, 161

Language and Biology Correlation, 51
Lesson Plan, 62
Lecture Method, 72
- importance, 72
- steps involved, 72
- when to use, 73
- merits, 74
- demerits, 74
- improving, 74

Lecture cum Demonstration
- method, 77
- steps, 77

Local School trips, 203
Logical Order Method of Curriculum Organisation, 181-82

M

Manipulation, 41
Manipulative and Observation Test in Labs, 161
Matching items test, 257
Materials and Activities Unit Plan, 61
Mathematics and Biology Correlation, 51
Medical stream preparing, 20
Method of Teaching, 69
Mock ups, 196
Model
concept for describing, 127
Models of Teaching in Families, 125
Modern Biology preference, 21
Molecular Biology, 21
- future, 24

Moral Value of Biology, 45
Motion Pictures, 198
M.Sc.
- subjects, 20
- integrated, programme, 21

Motion Pictures, 198
Multiple Choice tests, 256
Museums, 203

N

Nature
- understanding, 17

Natural Science, 27
Naturalization, 42
Newsreels, 200
Norm Referenced Test (NRT), 246
- /CRT differences, 247

Nuffield Biology Project, 188
Nurturant Effects, 148

O

Objectives of
- biology teaching domain, 35
- Unit Plan, 61

Objective type items, 257
- advantages/ disadvantages, 258

Optional Activities
- for students, 59
- in unit plan, 61

Osmosis Experiment Inquiry Approach, 105-106
Overhead Projector (OHP), 198

P

Paper Pencil test, 256
Parallel Courses for average/ above average students, 186
Partist Strategy of Reception Thinking, 140
Personal Models, 126
Phototropism lesson model class XI, 133-35
Physics and Biology

Correlation, 50
Ph.D, 20
integrated programme, 21
Physical Sciences, 27
Planning
- meaning, 53
- requirements, 53
- importance, 54
- types, 55

Pupil Centred Method of Teaching, 69
Post laboratory discussion, 153-54
Principles of Reaction, 128, 131
Problems pertaining to biology– integrated approach with other sciences, 33
Problem Solving Approach, 114
- Advantages, 114
- Disadvantages, 115
- teachers role, 114

Process dimension of cognitive domain
- structure, 39

Process films, 199
Programme (NCERT) for
- 11 year schooling, 189
- + 2 system, 190

Projectors, 197
Project Method, 90
- importance, 90
- steps, 90
- selection of project, 91
- planning, 91
- execution, 91
- evaluation, 91
- merits/demerits, 92
- teachers role, 92

Properties of Metals (teaching of), 106
Psychomotor
- Domain, 41, 43
- Objectives, 43

Psychological Value of Biology, 45

Q

Question Bank, 60
Question
- types, 60
- levels, 60

R

Radio, 197
Reception Thinking, 140
- strategies, 140
- model of teaching, 141
- syntax, 141-42, 145
- principles of, 143
- support/application, 143

Record Book (labs), 163
- evaluation, 163

Recording/Report (Project Method), 91
Recommendation for conservation, implementation, 32
References for students/ teachers, 66
Reproduction and family planning (teaching of), 32
Research Institution in India, 22
Revision films, 199

S

School level biology teaching scenario, 30
School Made Films, 199
Science Club, 214
- Aims, 215
- meaning, 214
- principles of, 214
- activities, 216
- and class room activities, differences, 214
- movement in India, 215
- organising, 217

- constitution, 218
- teachers role, 219
- teachers interest, 219
- curriculum, 219

Science
- types, 27
- Museum, 220
  - origin, 220
  - in school, 220
  - importance of, 221

Scientific attitude development of, 46
Secondary level biology, 19-20
Selection Thinking Strategies (CAM), 139
Searching Strategies, 140
Seasonal Arrangement of lessons – Method of Curriculum Development, 182-83
Simultaneous/Successive Scanning, 140
Slide Projectors, 197
Social Interaction Models, 126
Social System, 130
Social and Physical environment and Biology correlation, 52
Specific objectives, 33
STS (Science, Technology and Society)
- Approach, 108
- Merits, 109

Static Model, 196
Still Projection, 197
Subject Matter Unit Plan, 61
Summative Tests, 247
Support System, 128
Sustaining Biology factors, 19, 26
Systems Approach
- meaning, 116
- characteristics, 117
- uses, 118

System designing steps, 118
System Analysis steps, 118
Synthesis (cognition), 38

T

Tape Recorders, 197
Teaching/Research profession as career, 24
Teaching of biology
- objectives, 29, 33 at Sec/HS level, 29

Teacher centred method of teaching, 69
Teacher/learner controlled method of teaching – differences, 71
Teacher Made Achievement Test, 248
Teacher Role in Assignment Method, 83
Teacher's Guide, 189
Teaching Aids
- importance of, 193
- principles of, 194
- classification of, 195

Television, 200
Teleological Approach, 119
- Analysis, 119
- in teaching Bio/Physical Sciences, 121

Terarium
- meaning/setting up, 236
- in schools, 236
- Advantages, types, role of students, 237

Test construction steps involved, 253
Theatre, 202
Three Dimensional (3D) Material, 196
Title Page (Unit Plan), 61
Topic Method of Curriculum

Organization, 181
Training Value of Biology, 45
True Coelomates teaching lesson class XI, 144
True/False items test, 251

U

UGC
- proposals, 26
- research aid, 22

Universities/research institutions in India, 22
Unit meaning, 58
Unit Plan, 58
- rational, 58
- specifying content, 58
- advantages, 60
- components, 61

Unit Plan (Natural Resources), 67-68
Utilitarian value of Biology, 44

V

Value of Biology, 44
Video Programme, 200
Viva-voce in tab tests, 163
Vivarium
- meaning, making, 238
- advantages, 238-39

Vocational value of biology, 44

W

White boards, 196
Wholist (strategy of reception thinking), 140
Working model, 196

Y

Yellow Evolutionary Approach (BSCS), 186